The
Grand Acquisitors

The

Grand Acquisitors

John L. Hess

With Illustrations

HOUGHTON MIFFLIN COMPANY BOSTON

1974

Library of Congress Cataloging in Publication Data

Hess, John L
The grand acquisitors.

1. Hoving, Thomas Pearsall Field, 1931–
2. New York (City). Metropolitan Museum of Art.
I. Title.
N610.H47   069'.092'4   73–22021
ISBN 0–395–18013–9

Printed in the United States of America

To Adelaide Milton de Groot

who so wanted to have her
name in a piece of original historic research that she left her
fortune for that purpose, but
never achieved it until now

To the Odalisque in Gray

an enchanting lady whose fair
name is herein restored.

The old pot, put together with plaster,
Is really a scandalous disaster.
Why can't the trustees
Get off their knees
And de-accession their master?

Limerick by a staff member of the Met

Acknowledgments

The sources of information in this book are the standard ones of the reporter: legwork, interviews, a study of published materials. Valuable data were given me by critics and scholars, art dealers and donors, and fellow journalists. But to thank them by name here would be unjust to many who felt obliged to request anonymity, lest they suffer reprisals in their professions or businesses. I refer particularly to a number of devoted employees of the Metropolitan Museum of Art, who defied an order that no staff member speak to me. The revelations recounted here could not have been made without their help. I can think of no better argument for the reporter's right to protect his sources, a right that is now under grave attack.

My thanks to all.

J.L.H.

Contents

The

Grand Acquisitors

A Watergate in Art

Trustees are gladly suffered as highly ornamental, and occasionally useful, sacred cows to be milked on sight. But God forbid that they should have ideas on art beyond their station, for if they ever got the upper hand, the public, whose cross-section they represent, might question the omniscience of the expert.

— Francis Henry Taylor, director of the
Metropolitan Museum of Art from 1940 to
1954, quoted by Russell Lynes

Early in 1973, between the Christmas bombing of North Vietnam and the explosion of the Watergate affair, a series of scandals set the art world on its ear. Day after day, *The New York Times* spun out revelations about the Metropolitan Museum of Art, the greatest cultural treasure house of the Western Hemisphere. And what stories they were — about secret and peculiar deals involving millions of dollars in art, about the wooing and betrayal of an eccentric spinster heiress, about masterpieces called fakes and fakes called masterpieces, about stolen treasures, elusive dealers, tomb robbers, a chair mender in Zurich and a coin trader in Beirut . . . a cast of characters to make a novelist dream.

It was not only a rattling good yarn; it was important. It told a great deal about our society, the law, how contemporary and classic art is marketed, how museums are run and how archaeological treasures are looted. It brought to the fore the question of whether or not tax-supported institutions should continue to operate without public supervision. It also forced the administration of our greatest museum to raise, if only a little, the curtain of secrecy cloaking its operations and to halt, if belatedly, the sale of many important paintings and the remnant of a great coin collection that was vanishing into the hands of private collectors abroad.

Yet the museum administration was able to confuse the issues a bit with the allegation that the scandals were simply a "vendetta" by the *Times*, or more specifically by John Canaday and myself, against Director Thomas P. F. Hoving. (Just so, the White House was able to blunt the Watergate scandal in the summer and fall of 1972 with the allegation that the *Washington Post* was out to get President Nixon. The rest of the media generally held off; as Katharine Graham, publisher of the *Post*, has recalled of the period when only her newspaper was linking the Watergate burglary to the White House, "It got awfully lonesome.")

The press does on occasion expose wrongdoing in government. What it almost never does is expose the follies of museum trustees. For example, the great dealers' raid on the Minneapolis Institute of Arts (see Chapter XIV) and similar if lesser scandals at the Rhode Island School of Design will not be found in local newspaper files. It is hardly surprising that the media overlook stories unflattering to trustees, since their owners are often among them. My own employer, Arthur O. Sulzberger, is a member of the Acquisitions Committee of the Met. (I should add that he at no time intervened in my reporting, even as it repeatedly brought to light negligence on the part of his committee.)

The board of a museum is often a better guide to the local power structure than the Social Register.* Member-

* As might be expected, the board of our greatest museum is a power-house indeed, including such luminaries as C. Douglas Dillon and

ship is a badge of status, and the obligations it entails are generally honorary, untaxing and, on the whole, rather enjoyable. Mrs. Vincent Astor, a devoted and generous trustee of the Met, considered her duty well done when, on receiving a complaint from a prominent art authority and collector, she replied:

> I can quite understand your frustration in your experiences at the Metropolitan Museum, however, as a Trustee I have little or no influence in the administration and I am simply sending your letter on to Mr. Hoving, with a notation from me.
>
> Sincerely,
BROOKE ASTOR

This note is a wonderful specimen of the properly trained trustee's sense of inferiority to museum directors and curators. "In a way," confessed Francis T. P. Plimpton, "it makes no sense for museums to be run by me and people like me. I'm no expert on art. But the museum is pretty darned good, and we're trying to do the best job we can."

The trustees *know* they are ignorant about art; they *think* their employees are experts in every aspect of it. This puts a strong-minded director in a position of power unknown to other executives in our society. Even the chairman of a large corporation has the S.E.C. and Ralph Nader to contend with; he must keep records open to inspection and comply with laws on disclosure. Museum trustees, in contrast, jealously guard the secrecy of their actions and accept virtually no limits on their powers, which they in fact delegate to their directors.

Joseph Richardson Dilworth, banker-statesmen; Richard S. Perkins, André Meyer and David Schiff, bankers; Roswell L. Gilpatric, Robert Morgan Pennoyer and Francis T. P. Plimpton, corporation lawyers; Governor Nelson A. Rockefeller (honorary trustee); Charles B. Wrightsman, oil multimillionaire; Mayor John V. Lindsay, and so on. See page 31.

Senator Ervin has remarked that evil loves darkness, meaning that the secrecy that blanketed White House operations encouraged the most unlawful excesses. How could this be different in the art world? The concealment of museum transactions, the pretension of directors to total expertise, and the dizzy inflation of art values — all have vastly increased temptation to folly and worse, the more so since trustees, despite their wealth, are often tight with the dollar where salaries are concerned. (Curators, on average, earn less than truck drivers.)

As a result, there is probably no single major museum (not to mention the minor ones) without its intriguing catalogue of sins, recounted with amusement by the cognoscenti. But the public, which in the end picks up the tab, is hardly ever let in on the fun and games.

This time, for once, it was. Not on the whole story, but part of it. Enough to shock the public and bewilder the trustees. Mrs. Lee Seldes has reported that a board member's wife, reading the *Times* at the breakfast table, asked: "Dear, what's going on at the museum? Didn't you ask any questions?" Reply: "I didn't know what questions to ask."

One of the first questions to be asked is: who was Thomas P. F. Hoving, and what were the contradictory qualities that caused him, on the one hand, to lead the Metropolitan Museum into a series of disasters and, on the other, to gain such an ascendancy over his trustees as to preserve his powers to the bitter end?

CHAPTER 2

The Green Years

The first year, I thought he was brilliant. Then I began to get terribly apprehensive.

Tom's not a liar — he's a fantasist. He says things he'd like to be so.

— Recollections by friends of Tom Hoving

Buried in newspaper morgues is a photograph that, even in these disillusioned nineteen seventies, stirs nostalgia: two tall, attractive young men — the newly elected mayor of New York City and his newly appointed parks commissioner — exuberantly splashing each other with oars on a pond in Central Park. It was at once more charming and (because it was intended to help make the park a fun place again) more worthy of public attention than the celebrated scene in Camelot when Arthur Schlesinger, Jr., was pushed into the swimming pool, dinner jacket and all.

The time was now the mid sixties, and the country, increasingly disillusioned with Lyndon Johnson, still cherished a guilty memory of the Kennedys. Inevitably, the press was already talking of the liberal John Lindsay as the Republican white hope, and of the still younger liberal Tom Hoving as a coming governor or senator, for openers. Lindsay and Hoving were at the peak of their careers, and it would be downhill from there on. But nobody realized it then.

New York needed their zest. The city was down at the heels, down at the mouth. (It still is, to be sure.) The parks, especially, deserted by a frightened citizenry, needed Hoving. And he came on with a rush, this medievalist curator on a motorbike, proclaiming a revolution on the grass. "The old rinkydink, hand-me-down stereotype of a park is out, OUT!" he cried. He was going to give the city "Central Park à Go-Go"; he would "make Coney Island magnetic"; he would stud New York with vestpocket play areas. A few of these things he began, in his brief term.

"Happenings" were big then, and the biggest began happening in Central Park: one day, 5000 kites (anyhow, a lot of kites) flew overhead; another day, 3000 daubers (anyhow, quite a few) smeared a block-long sheet of paper with paint; on weekends bicycles replaced cars on the park ways. And there, always, was this lanky, long-faced, grinning young man, kiting, daubing, pedaling, clowning in costume, romping on foam rubber, climbing the wall of a comfort station. It was great copy.

Mary Nichols of the *Village Voice* was then Hoving's press secretary. Recently, she recalled: "He was a sensational park commissioner. The Arsenal [park headquarters] needed a bomb dropped on it. He gave the whole city a sense of joie de vivre . . . The first year, I thought he was brilliant. Then I began to get terribly apprehensive."

Ms Nichols at first thought her young boss very shy, but soon she found him chortling over a reporter's nickname for him, "Thomas Publicity Forever Hoving." (His middle names are Pearsall Field.) "He courted publicity and would call up reporters himself," she said. "One day he would go on television and say we had thirty-eight vestpocket parks, and I would have to work up a list in case somebody should ask. We only had seven or eight at that point . . . I put it down at the time to exuberance."

A typical contretemps concerned a rubble-strewn lot in

the desolate slum wastelands of the South Bronx, where Lindsay and Hoving announced before the cameras that they were building a happy playground. A month later, community leaders complained that the rubble was still there. It turned out that nobody had given orders actually to do anything. (This was one of the earliest recorded displays of what was to become a familiar performance: the announcement of brilliant achievements while they were still projects in the fertile Hoving mind. In 1972, for example, Hoving told the Metropolitan's trustees he would bring the museum the first loan exhibition from the Hermitage in Leningrad. Actually, it went to the National Gallery in Washington and Knoedler's in New York.)

When he proposed to open the Central Park reservoir to swimming, and the water commissioner retorted that the public needed the water for drinking, Hoving replied that one was permitted to "quack a little about some visionary ideas." He could be sharper when crossed. A park conservator who pleaded that some green areas be left in tranquillity was publicly savaged as a "fuddy-duddy." And at a "happening" in Central Park, when a reporter pressed Hoving to say who was picking up the tab for the party, he snapped, "None of your business!"

(Curiously, these were among the first words Hoving addressed to me seven years later, when I called to inquire about the fate of the missing *Odalisque*. The phrase, however, is more representative of his temper than of his command of language, which can be outstanding — to wit, his revival of the old Scottish word "kerfuffle," or "fuss," to describe the scandals at the museum.* Hoving could have made a brilliant career in some medium where color is more prized than accuracy.)

Hoving apologized to the reporter that day, though he

---

* In a similar situation, President Nixon could only describe the Watergate burglary as "a deplorable incident."

did not say where the money had come from. The press harbored no grudge. Few young men entering public life can have enjoyed a more enthusiastic and uncritical reportage. On his appointment as parks commissioner, Hoving was described by the *Times* as "a dashing man of action who flits around town on a Jawa motorcycle and eats meatball hero sandwiches." This first of many Hoving profiles continued: "He has a fey sense of humor, is a noted ocean yacht racer and is described as a delightful person to work with." And when, a year later, it was announced that Hoving would abandon the parks to return to the museum as director, *Newsweek* trumpeted, "The Met has chosen a winner."

It is curious, in reading the profiles of that period, to remark how material that could be devastating in the hands of a malicious or even skeptical biographer can be softened by a sympathetic one. Thus, all the accounts of Hoving's slugging the Latin teacher at Exeter who had given him an A-minus are careful to note that the teacher was 6 feet 5 — two inches taller than Hoving. Similarly, a party at Edgartown that ended in the burning of a town bulldozer, and a party at Princeton that saw a piano fed, piece by piece, into a fireplace, are related as youthful high jinks. Which no doubt they were . . .

While the pranks of the young rich have always been treated with more indulgence than, say, the scrawling of graffiti on subways and buses by slum children — an outrage that Mayor Lindsay could never suppress despite countless arrests — Hoving surely deserved the sympathy of his interviewers. He was himself the primary source of these anecdotes, and he described a troubled childhood and adolescence with considerable candor.

He did not conceal, for example, his difficult relationship with his father, Walter Hoving, a native of Sweden who had made his way up in retailing to the top of Bonwit

Teller, and later of Tiffany. Tom Hoving told a *Times* reporter: "He made me terribly aware of what it means to be responsible, and he did it through real fear. He's really a very imposing man."

His socialite mother, the former Mary Osgood Field, was different. "I guess there was a certain aspect of Auntie Mame about her," Tom said. The parents separated in 1936, when Tom was five years old, and, he related, "the divorce hit me pretty hard."

Tom and his sister, Petrea, stayed with their mother on Park Avenue. On weekends and some holidays, the children would visit their father, who had remarried. These appear to have been awkward occasions; Tom is said to have been difficult toward his stepmother. He was, on the other hand, deeply attached to his mother and his sister (for whom he would name his only child), although according to the definitive Profile in *The New Yorker*, their relationship was marked by "conflagrational fights."

Tom's record in school was the classic one of a bright but disturbed child. He attended four: Buckley, which "phased me out" in fourth grade as "needing individual attention"; Eaglebrook, which described him as having made "an excellent social adjustment" and "a good healthy amount of trouble"; Exeter, which expelled him after six months for unruly behavior, culminating in the incident with the Latin teacher, and Hotchkiss, where he achieved good grades but was remembered as introverted and withdrawn and was nicknamed Schmo.

The Profile says, a little cryptically, "Tom eventually learned not to participate — to act, when something unpleasant came up, as if it weren't there." Long afterward, a Park Avenue lady who knew him well put it more plainly, if still kindly: "Tom's not a liar — he's a fantasist. He says things he'd like to be so."

A softening view of his school experience was imparted

by Hoving to a *Times* interviewer, who found a bit of Holden Caulfield in the young Tom. Hoving said: "I've always had a broad streak of insubordination, I don't know why. I've always suspected the school spirit, cheering at football games, the old rah-rah — unless you really felt it. I never really got along at Hotchkiss, but I guess it was there that I realized that happiness was not the deal; the goal was to *do* something, to get *engaged* in something."

Princeton may be the last of Ivy League colleges where the tradition of the gentleman's C persisted, and there, what with cardplaying and drinking and cutting classes, Hoving said, "I really fell apart." Then he attended a seminar in art history and, as a friend put it, "It was as if he had found religion." His wife, Nancy, recalled more flippantly: "He was going to be an artist. He kept telling me . . . he was going to live an artist's life and I couldn't stand it. You know, up in a garret. Oh, too corny."

Anyway, Hoving straightened out and was graduated summa cum laude. This achievement seems hardly to have softened Walter Hoving, who was apparently no more elated at having a son in the arts than he had been at having a son twice kicked out of school. On graduation day, according to Tom, his father gave him $1000 and said: "There. That's all you'll ever get from me."

Hoving married and joined the Marines. While he was serving his hitch as a lieutenant, his mother died, leaving him an annual income of $5200. After a year in Italy with his bride, he returned to Princeton on a fellowship and emerged in 1959 with a doctorate in art history and a job as an assistant curator of medieval art at the Metropolitan Museum.

It was from that post that Hoving set out two years later on an adventure that in an extraordinary way foreshadowed all that was to come.

CHAPTER 3

Hoving's Cross

"The museum has never done anything illegal, and you had better believe that. We are no more illegal in anything we have done than Napoleon was when he brought all those treasures to the Louvre."

— Thomas Hoving to John McPhee of *The New Yorker*

By common consent, Hoving's reputation as an art scholar rests chiefly on his "discovery and identification" of what the Met describes as one of its greatest treasures, the cross of Bury St. Edmunds. Hoving often recalled this feat, in extraneous contexts, as a model of acquisition and enrichment of the collection. In an interview during the 1973 scandals, he complained that his achievement ten years earlier had not got the play it deserved. It is time to make up for the oversight.

Actually, there are as many published reports of the "discovery and identification" as there are sketches of Hoving, and they all agree on the main points — as they should, since all come from the same source. The longest and best is the one in *The New Yorker* Profile of Hoving by his Princeton classmate John McPhee, which combines the suspense of a spy thriller with the exaltation of a lone researcher finding the cure to a mysterious plague.

From a curator friend in Boston, the story goes, Hoving learned that a collector named Ante Topic-Mimara (a "former Tito partisan," in the official history of the Metropolitan Museum by Calvin Tomkins) had a magnificently carved ivory cross in a bank vault in Zurich. It was generally suspected to be a fake, but Hoving wanted to see for himself.

He told McPhee that in that "subterranean" vault, in 1961, the stocky, swarthy little Yugoslav, "with a stubble, slightly hunched shoulders, a rapid walk, slightly turned-in feet, darkish hair and a face like a crowd," tantalized the tall, clean-cut young American by reserving the cross while showing him, one by one, a treasure of art objects — what remained of the contents of two boxcars he had got out of Berlin after the war, "with the complicity of an American colonel." Finally, Topic-Mimara removed a black cloth to reveal the cross.

Hoving had the habit, he told McPhee, of writing down on a scrap of paper his first impression of an art object; that first hunch, he had found, was generally right. This time he scribbled, "No doubt." It was not only a genuine carving of about the twelfth century, it was "staggering, a truly great, great thing." What Hoving saw was a cross of walrus ivory a bit less than two feet tall and just over a foot wide, covered with tiny enchanting Romanesque figures and inscriptions in Latin and Greek.

Hoving spent three days in the vault, gazing at the cross, with Topic-Mimara beside him reading newspapers. Only once did the Yugoslav step out for a moment, taking Hoving's camera with him — there were to be no photographs. Well-prepared for this opportunity, Hoving thereupon whipped a tiny Minox from his pocket and snapped away. (He bragged about this to some trustees, who are said to have considered it pretty cute.)

Hoving showed the pictures to two leading authorities on medieval ivories, and they agreed the cross was authentic. But Topic-Mimara was asking "well over £200,000"

— more than $500,000* — for the ivory, and the Met trustees were hesitant. They stalled for a year. Then James J. Rorimer, the director, learned that the British Museum was interested in the cross (in fact, it had obtained an option), and he told Hoving to fly to Zurich. "There is a sense of timing in this sort of thing," Hoving said to McPhee. "A museum man has to sense when to wait things out, when to bluff and when to move fast."

Hoving arrived in Zurich one winter day in early 1963 with ski boots under his arm. The disguise does not seem to have fooled Rupert L. S. Bruce-Mitford of the British Museum, who passed him in the hotel lobby. The Briton said coolly, "Well, Mr. Hoving, I imagine you feel something like Paul Revere." Nevertheless, Bruce-Mitford did not meet the option deadline — "apparently," so McPhee was led to believe, "because the Exchequer would not approve of a sterling drain as heavy as Topic-Mimara's price." The morning after the British option expired, Hoving handed over a check and took the ivory.

Then, in New York and Princeton, as Hoving told it, he pored over archives hunting for medieval art similar to the carvings on the cross. From hundreds of photographs, he culled out seven; two were of unknown origin and five were identified with the town of Bury St. Edmunds, site of a once rich and powerful monastery. "Hoving deciphered the sixty-three Greek and Latin inscriptions on the cross," McPhee tells us. He put them together and found they amounted to an anti-Semitic tract, denouncing the Jews for

---

* I am unable to confirm this figure. The British say the price put on them was £200,000 flat. A Metropolitan source says this is somewhat exaggerated. The museum has traditionally declined to say how much it has paid for art objects not obtained at public auction. Hoving, acutely aware of the enhancement that high prices lend to public appreciation of the arts, has been known to encourage inflated reports, as in the affair of the Euphronios vase.

the rejection and murder of Christ. (As in many church carvings of the period, the Jews in the scenes on the cross are identified as such by their conical hats.)

Pursuing his hunt to England, Hoving learned that there had been a particularly virulent fever of anti-Semitism at Bury St. Edmunds from 1182 to 1190, culminating in the massacre of fifty-seven Jews, and that the campaign had been led by Abbot Samson, the harsh master of the monastery, who was then engaged in a power struggle with a more "Christian" faction.

In the Bury Bible, made in the twelfth century, Hoving said he found illuminated initials whose figures looked almost exactly like those on the cross. Our researcher went to Cambridge where, "at random, he removed a volume marked M-72 from the shelf." Lucky find. It was a twelfth-century copy of the Gospel of Mark, and where the Latin text of the placard on the Cross is corrctly rendered as "KING OF THE JEWS," an unknown hand had written in, "KING OF THE CONFESSORS" — that is, the true believers — explaining that this revision was called for by "the perfidy of the Jews." Now the Crucifixion scene carved on the ivory cross bears precisely this latter version: "IESUS NAZARENUS REX CONFESORUM."

"I had a long way to go," Hoving said, "but the matter was essentially solved with this discovery." The following year, he published his identification and analysis in the museum *Bulletin,* which added the good news that a missing plaque from the base had been hunted down and acquired . . .

Entertaining and edifying to the layman, nonetheless aspects of this story should stir up a certain uneasiness in a professional skeptic such as a scholar or a journalist. Hoving had "discovered and identified a famous 12th century ivory cross from Bury St. Edmunds, which had been ignored for several centuries," the *Times* said. Well, "discovery" is a fairly grand word for an appointment to look at an object in a bank vault, an object that was being offered for sale at "well over" half a million dollars, and on which the British Museum would obtain an option. The identification of the cross also seems on the face of it less than conclusive. Upon closer examination, the story as told by McPhee and others crumbles rapidly.

One learns, first, that Director Rorimer had known about the cross since 1956, some three years before he hired Hoving. Topic-Mimara had been peddling it to well-heeled museums. Under her maiden name, Wiltrud Mersmann, his wife had written a book-length paper on the cross, which was widely circulated in manuscript. (When the paper was published in 1963, with 94 illustrations and 210 footnotes, the acknowledgments showed she had consulted at least nineteen scholars on both sides of the Atlantic. Some "discovery"!)

Two of Rorimer's scouts — including the man who switched jobs and became the "friend in a museum in Boston" in the Hoving story — had actually visited the vault in Zurich. True, they were leery; the price was high and the cross looked "too good to be true." But it remained on Rorimer's mind. He was a medievalist himself; along with John D. Rockefeller III, he had built the museum's uptown shrine of medieval art, The Cloisters, which has been called the most nearly perfect little museum in the hemisphere. If the cross was genuine, Rorimer wanted to install it there.

At the same time, the shy and self-conscious Rorimer was enormously attracted to the socially secure and ebullient young Hoving, who brought an enthusiasm to the medieval department that the older man felt had been lacking. Already, the director was grooming his protégé for higher things. So when the time came to consider a serious bid for the cross, he sent Hoving over for another look at it.

Here the McPhee-Hoving saga overlooks a detail. Hoving was not, as all accounts imply, *alone* in that vault with Topic-Mimara for those three days. He had asked a senior associate, Carmen Gomez-Moreno, to lend an experienced eye. She did, and concurred that the cross was genuinely medieval. Miss Gomez-Moreno, now a full curator, testifies that Hoving took no pictures with a Minox or any other camera in that vault. The photograph shown to the Met trustees was in fact given Rorimer by Topic-Mimara the following year and came from the set illustrating Mrs. Topic-Mimara's learned paper. This helped to sway the board, if we may accept what Hoving told Richard Walter of *The Observer* long afterward: he argued that the couple would hardly be circulating such documents if the cross were counterfeit or stolen. That was, Hoving acknowledged, all the evidence he had.

In a note in the 1964 museum *Bulletin* saluting Hoving's "brilliant research," Rorimer mentioned Miss Gomez-Moreno's role and revealed that he himself had gone to Zurich in 1962 with Curator Margaret Freeman to study the cross, using ultraviolet rays "to assure ourselves of its antiquity." When he learned that the British (who did not seem to need Hoving's pictures or even Miss Gomez-Moreno's eye) were ready to meet Topic-Mimara's price, Rorimer sent Hoving over to outbid them, if possible, and to bring back the cross — with all the credit attached to it.

At this point, the account given by the British Museum people diverges from Hoving's. They had recognized the cross as a magnificent specimen of medieval art, very possibly English, and despite the monetary situation, they had persuaded the Exchequer to release the necessary funds. Their qualms were ethical, not financial. They wanted assurance that Topic-Mimara held an honest title to the object he was selling, and this the Yugoslav refused to give. To this day, he has never revealed where he got the cross.

Topic-Mimara's origins, it appears, were no clearer than those of the cross. The Tomkins-Hoving account describes him as a former Tito partisan who turned up in Berlin after the war, wearing a Yugoslav marshal's uniform. Yet Yugoslav diplomats in New York say Topic-Mimara was on the other side — no more a Tito partisan than Dikran Sarrafian, the Lebanese coin dealer in the affair of the Euphronios vase, who liked to pretend he had been a British agent parachuted to Tito's forces during the war.

A different though still lurid light on Topic-Mimara is shed by Heinz Höhne and the late Hermann Zolling of *Der Spiegel* in their study of the anti-Soviet spy organization headed by General Reinhard Gehlen, working first for Hitler, then for the C.I.A., and finally for Bonn. A Yugoslav agent captured in 1949 is quoted as having said "Head of the Yugoslav intelligence service in Germany is a certain Topic, alias Mimara, a museum custodian by profession. He is a member of the Yugoslav Restitution and Reparations Commission in the US Zone. In 1947 T. was expelled from Säckingen by the French for currency offences; he went first to Berlin and thence to Frankfort am Main; he is now in Munich." At any rate, the British had solid reasons to demand proof that the cross had not been stolen.

Hoving needed no more proof of title in 1963 than he did a decade later, when he bought the Euphronios vase. As Topic-Mimara and Hoving have both confirmed, the young American took no chance of missing out on the purchase. First he topped the British bid, and then he sat with the Yugoslav in a café until the British option expired at midnight. Five minutes later, the cross belonged to the Metropolitan Museum.

It is a tribute to Hoving's youthful charm that, in a world marked by jealousy and intrigue, he received extraordinary help and indulgence from elder colleagues. Rorimer not only minimized his own part in the "discovery" and purchase, but also assigned several staff members to aid Hoving in his research. Among them was a young Englishwoman specially hired to help translate and identify the Latin and Greek inscriptions. Scholars outside the museum also lent assistance, like the one who showed him the pictures in the Bury Bible. They winced when his paper appeared, announcing as *proven* what they accepted as *hypothesis* — that the cross came from Bury St. Edmunds. This, one of them said recently, is "arrogance, not scholarship."

Sabrina Longland, who studied the inscriptions for Hoving, was noncommittal about its origins in a paper she wrote for a Met publication. But in *Connoisseur* magazine, after her return to Britain, she published a new report titled "The 'Bury St. Edmunds Cross.'" Note the quotation marks. The cross, she wrote, had been dated "anywhere from around 1115 to as late as 1190"; "the Bury connections, although tempting, are not conclusive; on certain evidence it now looks as if they are simply coincidences, which fit the cross into an English or possibly Continental background in the second half of the twelfth century." Miss Longland found that the substitution of "King of the Confessors" for "King of the Jews" was not uncommon in medieval times and could be found in at least three other medieval manuscripts, one English, the others French.

Hoving had cited another line from the cross as corroborating evidence. It was a verse known to have been used by Abbot Samson on the screen of his painted choir. However, Miss Longland reported that the line used by Samson differed from the one on the cross, which corresponded instead to the version used in Paris.

Miss Longland nevertheless clung to the view that the cross was English. Some of her compatriots thought it probably came from Yorkshire, rather than Suffolk, but others said it could have been made in Cologne, on the Rhine, or in fact anywhere in Northern Europe. The latter hypothesis was buttressed, if anything, by a fine little ivory body of Christ that Hoving borrowed from the small Kunstindustrimuseet in Oslo. He mounted it on the cross and suggested that it might well be the missing original. The figure had been regarded as Norwegian, but some scholars were persuaded that it might belong to the same style and period as the cross. Further study, however, showed that the holes did not fit. A German scholar, W. Sauerlander, called it a mismate. In a review in *The Art Bulletin*, he declared that the Christ was clearly Gothic and a date before 1210 was "improbable," while the Cloisters cross was pure Romanesque "and may well be as early as 1150."

Like other scholars, Sauerlander also challenged the claim that the little plaque Hoving had "restored" to the base was part of the original. It was different not only in size and style, he pointed out, but also in substance, being of true ivory rather than of walrus tusk.

The museum's own catalogue for a 1970 centennial exposition, *The Year 1200*, opens with a foreword by Hoving that begins, typically, "During my months of research in 1963 and 1964 on the Bury St. Edmunds cross I became fascinated with . . . that exceptional period." But the learned editor of the catalogue, Dr. Konrad Hoffmann, felt obliged to give the origin of the cross as "Bury St. Edmunds (?)," mentioning that there were stylistic, historic and philological grounds to doubt Hoving's attribution. Since then, scholars have dropped the Bury St. Edmunds tag altogether; they now call it the Cloisters Cross.

So much for the "discovery and identification" of the "Bury St. Edmunds Cross."

For a final note to this story, we must go back to McPhee's *New Yorker* Profile. Not for the tale of the cross, but for a visit to the Hoving living room on the fashionable East Side, not far from the museum. The room contains, we learn, quite an eclectic collection of art, including a model of the cross and "a fifteenth-century Russian icon given to Hoving by Ante Topic-Mimara."

Had Rupert L. S. Bruce-Mitford returned to the British Museum with the cross and a gift from the seller — or even a purchase for his personal collection — he would have been dismissed immediately. Ethical standards of museums are more rigid in Britain than in the United States, but even here curators are not allowed to accept gifts from dealers.

Perhaps McPhee was mistaken.

CHAPTER 4

Pretenders and Rulers

> The arrogance and conceit of those people were phe-
> nomenal. They really felt they were the lords of creation,
> and that nobody had the right even to question what they
> did.
>
> — Former Parks Commissioner Robert Moses, describing
> the trustees of the Metropolitan Museum
> (quoted by Calvin Tomkins)

Early in 1964, Hoving confided to friends a sense of
failure. He had just turned thirty-three, and he remarked
that Alexander the Great had conquered the world before
he died at that age. For his part, Hoving had only achieved
his little triumph with the "Bury St. Edmunds Cross."

True, he had made what appeared in staid museum
circles as an Alexandrian rise: it was pretty clear that
Director Rorimer would soon jump his protégé over the
heads of stodgy seniors to manage his beloved Cloisters.
But what then? The director himself was a hale fifty-nine
years old, and assuming he retired at sixty-five there was no
good reason to believe that the trustees would again name a
curator from within the museum as new director; before
Rorimer, they had always gone outside.

Once the cross was "published," as the scholars say,
Hoving returned to his curatorial chores with typical en-
ergy, but, also typically, his attention soon strayed. For
several years, he had been sporadically active in promoting
the political career of his boating companion John Lindsay;

at the beginning of 1965, a mayoral election year, Hoving drew up for Lindsay an imaginative paper on how to revitalize the city parks. This led to an impressive television series on parks featuring young Tom. Amid the praise, complaints reached Rorimer that his young protégé was occupying the medieval department's phone and office with matters far from medieval. The director summoned Hoving and gently suggested that, the museum being a nonpartisan institution, he take leave if he wanted to participate in the election campaign. This Hoving did on the very day his appointment as head of The Cloisters became effective. "Jim knew Tom was a goner," a friend recalled recently. "It was a blow."

Rorimer was not surprised when Hoving came to him after the election and said he had been offered a city post. The older man replied, so the story goes, cryptically: "I know what *I* would do." Rorimer was deeply hurt, but would not interfere in a decision that might shape a man's career.

Hoving proved that the quickest way to the directorship was a fast turn around the park. As commissioner, he was suddenly the museum's landlord — the Parks Department owns and maintains the building, and pays its guards and custodians — and was an ex officio trustee. He joked about being Rorimer's boss now, but of course kept hands off. In this he followed a century-old tradition; no city official has ever stood up to the Metropolitan's board except the indomitable commissioner Robert Moses, who after the war decreed that the museum would have to pony up at least half the cost of new construction and who also blocked the trustees' idea for a wing to house the Whitney Museum as a plan for "another wart" on Central Park.

One night in May 1966 Rorimer died in his sleep. Hoving had then been at the Arsenal less than a year and a half, and his great program for giving New York a sparkling garland of happy parks was barely begun, but he decided almost immediately to switch jobs.* The suddenness was typical. As an admiring young woman aide of Hoving's told Grace Glueck of the *Times:* "Tom's fantastically decisive. He thinks fast and will give you a decision a minute. Of course, there are times when it's not the right one, but he never has trouble making up his mind."

It was not as if he were leaving politics for good. If the Parks Commission could be a springboard to the museum directorship — and Hoving himself later said that his parks record was crucial in winning him the job — then why should the directorship not be a steppingstone to bigger things? A bit later Ms Glueck quoted Hoving as admitting that the Met was "a kind of backwater," and she suggested that he was available for appointment as United States Secretary of Culture, a post he had recommended establishing. An old Park Avenue friend says Tom was aiming higher than the cabinet. "Tom's sad, in a way," this friend told me. "He could have been a great medievalist, but who wants to be a great medievalist when there's Washington?"

The decision once taken to become director of the Met, it remained for Hoving to obtain an invitation. One doesn't *apply* for such a job; one is cautiously sounded out about one's availability and receives such an approach with surprise and humility.

Rather remarkably, Hoving enlisted as a lobbyist a man who was himself being mentioned in the press as a potential

---

* His timing was perhaps better than was generally appreciated at the time. Disillusion was beginning to set in among some of the park commissioner's backers. A couple of years afterward, an editorial in the *Times* suggested that Hoving had forgotten that Central Park was, after all, a park and should not become "a concrete-covered playground or an open-air walk-in theater." Hoving had offended the editorialist by calling a park defender a "fuddy-duddy."

successor to Rorimer. This unlikely John Alden was the curator of paintings, Theodore Rousseau, Jr. He had the necessary seniority and experience and was probably better liked by the trustees than any other member of the staff. But nobody seems to have taken Rousseau seriously as a candidate for the directorship. Not even Ted Rousseau himself.

Any institution dependent on the charity of the rich, and especially of the olderly female rich, would count itself lucky to have a Ted Rousseau on its staff. Dark, handsome, attentive, and sophisticated in a weary Charles Boyer manner, he was the perfect escort for the distinguished guest. He was born for the job: half-French son of a Morgan banker in Paris, attended the elite Ecole Henri IV, Eton, Harvard College and the Sorbonne; served a pleasant war as a United States Naval attaché in Lisbon and Madrid. Rousseau then spent a year or so with an OSS team, which included Rorimer, that was hunting for art looted by the Nazis. Finally, he obtained a job with the Met in 1947.

Biographies list him as unmarried, overlooking a sophomoric escapade of his Harvard days, when newspapers reported his wedding to a showgirl under the quaint headline: BANKER'S SON ELOPES. His father got the marriage annulled and Ted never repeated the error. As a bachelor, he became a highly desirable figure in New York society — an attractive unattached male to fill out a dinner party.

Another asset was his charming, amoral, altogether Parisian wit. A curator who accused him of a stab in the back says Ted replied with an urbane smile, "Today I betray one man, tomorrow another." And the art historian John Rewald recalls that when he turned down a request by Rousseau to help organize a loan exhibition from a multimillionaire collector, on the ground that the paintings were unworthy of the Met, Ted retorted, "That's the kind of hypocrisy I have been fighting all my life."

Rousseau loved the partygoing, the courtship of elderly heiresses like Adelaide de Groot, the intrigue within the museum, the wheeling and dealing with art merchants. What he found tiresome was the drudgery of curatorship; it was really quite unnecessary.

Perhaps the key to understanding the art world, if it can be understood at all, is pretension. Like the rest of the public, the typical trustee is reluctant to admit how little he really knows about art, or to suspect how limited is the expertise of his director and curators. In this kingdom of the blind, then, the one-eyed man is king.

Take the painting that the Met's house history (*Merchants and Masterpieces,* by Calvin Tomkins) describes as "Velazquez's stunning equestrian portrait of *Don Gaspar de Guzmán, Count Duke of Olivares.*" Ted Rousseau brought that one home in 1952, having bought it from the Earl of Elgin at a reported price of $207,200. The acquisition was greeted with a paean of hometown pride and esthetic ecstasy by *The New York Times.* Specialists were appalled, however. Their immediate impression that this was not a Velázquez was strengthened by further study and then published in the literature. The consensus now is that the portrait was most likely done by Velázquez's son-in-law, Juan Bautista del Mazo.

A curator of the Met, asked why this painting had not been included in the recent revision of labels of museum masterpieces, replied shamefacedly that it was "Rousseau's Velázquez." A good-humored fellow of the museum calls it "The Rockinghorse Velázquez," and indeed the fat white horse under the fat white knight does look rather like nursery furniture. But this may be a phenomenon of hindsight as described by Calvin Tomkins: "When the authenticity of a work of art is questioned, the object, if it is a fake, often just falls apart before the curatorial eye."

Tomkins was writing about the Greek *Bronze Horse,*

long a world-famous treasure of the Met, which was denounced as a forgery at a conference staged by Hoving with great éclat in 1967. Immediately, Tomkins said, the lovely bronze "began to look horribly wrong." However, some scholars refused to accept the evidence, and by 1972 they had produced conclusive proof that the horse was genuine after all. But Hoving was a man who could make hay in a downpour. Having landed on page one with the discovery that the horse was a fake, he now made page one by restoring it to the breed book, both times enhancing his reputation for scholarly honesty. He staged a special exhibition for the horse, in all its restored beauty, with legends contrasting the forgery charge (attributed exclusively, in huge illuminated signs, to Joseph V. Noble, a respected administrator who had left the museum in a dispute with Hoving) with the scientific findings that the piece was genuine. Nowhere in the show was there mention that the director and his curator of Greek and Roman art, Dietrich von Bothmer, had supported the "discovery" of the fake.

A comparable affair involves another Velázquez. In the midst of the 1973 art scandals, the Met revealed virtuously that it was downgrading the attributions of many paintings (not necessarily prior to selling them), and it was widely credited with a disarming honesty in so doing. The most prominent of the demoted canvases was the portrait of Philip IV, which curator Everett Fahy declared could not have been done by Velázquez, offering learned proof relating to the costume and a medal. Top experts such as José Lopez-Rey promptly shot down Fahy's proof and rehabilitated the Velázquez. So at this writing, if the experts are right, the museum is hanging a non-Velázquez as a Velázquez, and a Velázquez as a non-Velázquez. Truly, the painter seems to have cast an evil eye on the Met.

Playing this game of truth or consequences fascinated Hoving. Talking to John McPhee of *The New Yorker*, he had said, "I love forgeries!" and he claimed to have made an ivory once that fooled four out of five experts. To detect fakes he said: "Your eye is king. Get in touch with other scholars — everybody you think is expert [advice he failed to follow in the case of the Greek horse and many others] . . . Max Friedländer, the great art historian, once said, 'It may be an error to buy a work of art and discover that it is a fake, but it is a sin to call a fake something that is genuine.' "

Rorimer himself could be taken in when he strayed from his own specialty of medieval art; there was an Albani he bought on the spur of the moment in Rome, which was recently quietly sold as a copy. Hoving and Rousseau, however, shared a claim to eclectic expertise covering the range of the museum's interests. Both had appropriate social backgrounds, both enjoyed the game of cultivating trustees, both loved the acquisition of treasures of great price. Why Rousseau, the senior curator, decided to further Hoving's career is not clear; intimates think Ted knew he was liked but not sufficiently respected by the trustees to have a chance. In any case, his deference did not go unrewarded. He was subsequently named a vice director and curator in chief. He was, in fact, the only member of Rorimer's top team to survive.

Hoving's election was a breeze. He arrived at the board meeting with a few scribbled notes and launched into what appears to have been a brilliant two-hour presentation: as he'd done with the parks, he was going to bring the Met to the people and vice versa; the old pile was going to swing with the sixties.

The staid trustees must have felt rejuvenated — and reassured. This was the time of our cultural revolution: no city seemed immune from the flames of race violence, the campuses were in ferment, the Theater of the Absurd, the "happening" and Pop Art were threatening the eternal cultural verities. The backlash had not yet arrived. What better way to save the house than to put it in the hands of a young rebel of sound background?

CHAPTER 5

Tavern in the Red

> What should we really do, as responsible revolution-
> aries (and I consider myself one), as reasonable rebels
> (and I consider myself a rebel)? I'll give you Hoving's
> Law: Fight, challenge and struggle, but — this is the
> subparagraph of the law and very important — become
> the Establishment and beat the Establishment at its own
> game. Not by attacks and constant criticism or abrasive
> chatter all the time, but by getting into the Establishment
> and changing it by sweet reason and perhaps even
> honeyed persuasion.
>
> — Thomas Hoving, in his 1968 commencement address
> at Bennington College

Hoving began his career as director of the Met as he had
begun as parks commissioner, like a house afire. Before his
first year was out, he had expanded the administration by
hiring or promoting twenty-six executives, mostly young;
announced a change in emphasis from the preservation and
display of art to education and decentralization; set up a
contemporary arts department to install the Met in a field
then occupied by three other New York museums; landed
for the Met three great prizes, each worthy of a museum in
its own right; bought his first art object of record price, the
$1.4 million Monet *Terrasse à Ste.-Adresse,* and put the
museum deep in the red for the first time since the Depres-
sion (he would keep it there through his regime). Before
the second year was out, he had also managed to alienate
conservationists, architects, Jews, blacks, critics, artists, art
lovers and a large segment of the museum staff.

While other museum directors have been involved in controversy, it is probable that none before had been involved in such an unbroken series of controversies and scandals, nor had offended so large a sector of the public. Never before, for example, had the Met been permitted to sink into permanent deficit and its membership and attendance to slump.

Each succeeding crisis raised the question: how can Hoving survive? One obvious answer was that, as Robert Moses had put it, the trustees "really felt that they were the lords of creation, and that nobody had the right even to question what they did." Furthermore, each time they defended their director against the commonalty, their prestige became more involved with his. There was, as will be seen, a strong club spirit among them; no member cared to offend another, and if one were caught cheating at cards, no word of it might be allowed to seep abroad.*

Hoving's exploitation of the strengths and weaknesses of the trustees was exemplary. One of his first acts as director was to call on Robert L. Lehman, the estranged vice president of the museum. Head of a family of bankers and connoisseurs, Lehman owned one of the world's greatest art collections, today valued at upwad of $150 million. He was only the second Jew to have been elected to the board of the Met, and he became its most knowledgeable and one of its most devoted members. "Bobby," one of his relatives recalled recently, "was terribly sensitive about being Jew-

---

* As illustrated by this museum anecdote: Dietrich von Bothmer, the curator, once asked the Acquisitions Committee to buy a rather expensive piece. Excluded from their deliberations, he was later advised that he had been turned down. Mrs. Brooke Astor apologized to him prettily: "Charlie Wrightsman was against it, and I was going to spend the weekend with the Wrightsmans in Florida, so I couldn't vote *for* it." But the story has a happy ending. A bit later, Mrs. Astor quietly gave von Bothmer the money to buy the work.

ish, and he deeply appreciated being admitted into a world where Jews once were not welcome."

It had long been expected that his collection would go to the Met. But in 1964, when the Wall Street lawyer Roland L. Redmond retired as president, the board passed over Lehman, his logical successor, in favor of Arthur A. Houghton, Jr., of Corning Glass (later succeeded by C. Douglas Dillon). Deeply hurt, Lehman withdrew from active participation in the Met and decided to leave his treasure to his own private museum on West Fifty-fourth Street. According to Calvin Tomkins, his only contact with the museum after that snub was the faithful attendance of Ted Rousseau.

Hoving quickly ended the estrangement. He created the honorary post of chairman of the board for Lehman. The banker readily forgave and forgot. When he died in 1969, he left his art to the museum, with an endowment for its maintenance, on condition that a separate wing be erected to house it.

On similar terms, Hoving persuaded Governor Nelson Rockefeller to give the Met his collection of primitive art, to be displayed in a wing bearing the name of Rockefeller's son Michael, who had disappeared on an expedition in New Guinea.

Hoving already enjoyed close ties with Mayor Lindsay, one of three city officials who are ex officio trustees of the Met. Also on the board, then or soon thereafter, were:

- C. Douglas Dillon — former head of Dillon, Read and Company; Republican leader of the draft-Eisenhower movement who became John F. Kennedy's secretary of the treasury; intimate of the Rockefellers; former chairman of the Harvard Board of Overseers
- Roswell L. Gilpatric — like Dillon a political swing man, a Democratic backer of the Republican Nelson Rocke-

feller and the Democrat J. F. Kennedy; former deputy secretary of defense; a lawyer and corporation director described as having "more connections than an IBM computer"

- Joseph Richardson Dilworth (Met vice president) — banker now with Rockefeller Family and Associates; director of several corporations; trustee of many institutions
- André Meyer — head of Lazard Frères and Company; so much an intimate of the Kennedys that Jackie's marriage to Onassis was described by a quipster as another Lazard merger
- Robert Morgan Pennoyer — lawyer and member of the J. P. Morgan family; like Gilpatric, a former Pentagon official and, like Gilpatric and Dilworth, a member of the Council on Foreign Relations

Also, Arthur Houghton, Jr., of Corning Glass, president and then chairman of the Met; Charles B. Wrightsman, oil multimillionaire; David Schiff of Kuhn, Loeb (where Dilworth long toiled); Arthur Ochs Sulzberger, publisher of *The New York Times;* Francis T. P. Plimpton, former president of the New York City Bar Association, et cetera.

With trustees like these, the new director of the Met could airily tell a *Times* interviewer: "Our board is one of the greatest in the United States, but there are people not on it who should be on." He proceeded to enlarge the board steadily, from twenty-eight to thirty-six members. As will be seen, a few of the old members occasionally became restive, but the new ones, grateful to Hoving and Dillon for their social elevation, were steadfast in their loyalty.

Another early coup by Hoving was the acquisition of the Temple of Dendur. Egypt had offered it to the United

States in gratitude for contributions toward the rescue of Abu Simbel. Others wanted it, notably the Smithsonian and the Kennedy family, who hoped to have it erected beside the Kennedy Center on the Potomac. But dampness threatened the old stones, and Hoving won them with his plan for a glass enclosure in the park behind the Met.

There were objections on various grounds, including the esthetic, but Hoving retorted that it would make a great piece of walk-in sculpture. "The quality of the temple is not high," he told Grace Glueck of the *Times*, "but don't knock it. Its impact is extraordinary."

In the course of these operations, Hoving's love for the trappings of cloak-and-dagger intrigue (such as his ski disguise on the trip to Zurich) took a curious turn. He told friends he had taped a telephone conversation with Mrs. Jacqueline Kennedy, who insisted on having the temple as a memorial on the Potomac "even if it falls into dust." And at dinner one evening, he reminded art historian William C. Seitz of a phone chat they had had about the value of the Monet *Terrasse*, and said he had played the tape for trustees to persuade them to meet the price. Seitz is still outraged.

A former official of the museum insists that no such tape was ever so employed. But Hoving seemed to like people to *think* he played such games. Unfortunately, this illusion finally took hold. In my own investigations, those staff members courageous enough to talk to me would leave the museum and ring me from a pay booth.

Hoving was well on his way to making the Met the largest museum in the world, larger even than the Louvre, with the addition of the Temple of Dendur, the Rockefeller museum, the Lehman Pavilion and the forthcoming $15 million American Bicentennial Wing — all the while preaching a fashionable "decentralization" of the Met into the five boroughs. This expansionism led to the first of a series of kerfuffles that would shake the museum from within and without. They are worth summarizing here, for they were a preparation for the greater scandals to come.

Lovers of the park awoke to the fact that Hoving's "Master Plan," as he called it, would take from the greensward behind the Met a space equal to the existing building. They fought a long battle in the courts but got nowhere; Hoving was able to show that the century-old free lease accorded by the city included the green area to be covered. All the museum wanted, he said, was "to build on our own property." (Murray Kempton observed in the *New York Review of Books* that this statement was "evidence of nothing except his achievement of the fighting pitch which enables a partisan to *feel* something that he *knows* is not true.")

Mayor Lindsay stood aside and Hoving's handpicked successor as parks commissioner, August Heckscher, Jr., went along with an encroachment that, everyone said, Hoving would never have permitted while *he* was parks commissioner.* The opposition did get a public hearing, where it pointed out that neither the Board of Estimate, nor the Arts Commission, nor the Parks Commission, nor even the Met trustees had yet approved the plan. (The

---

* In his commencement address at Bennington in 1968 — the year of the student revolt — Hoving commented that Columbia University might have been *legally* right in its effort to take a piece of Morningside Park for a gym, but "many people" thought it was "morally reprehensible." Hoving had in fact helped spark the opposition to the project, which was canceled after a violent uprising. In 1973 he told *New York* magazine that if he had been leading the opposition to the museum's expansion into Central Park, "I could probably have stopped the construction." He'd have used political pressure, he said. "Legal things sometimes don't make the difference," he explained; and, "That's the bottom line, isn't it?"

Landmarks Commission and the community opposed it.) Hoving brandished a document that he said was a warning from trustees of the Lehman Foundation that they'd give the collection to the National Gallery unless the Pavilion was built; the *Times* later canvassed the trustees and found none who had knowledge of such a threat.

When Mrs. Jessie McNab Dennis, an assistant curator of European arts, applauded an opponent, Hoving told her: "I've been watching you. It's obvious that you're unhappy at the museum." Afterward, he sent an aide to suggest she resign. Many other staff members accepted similar invitations during the Hoving years — including roughly half the department chiefs — but the intrepid Scotswoman declined. Instead, she helped organize a women's rights group and a staff association. The former, with the help of the state attorney general Louis J. Lefkowitz, obtained from the museum an agreement to bar discrimination against women in salaries and promotions. The staff association had a rougher time; in November 1972 the National Labor Relations Board accused the museum of having dismissed fifteen employees and established what amounted to company unions in an effort to discourage organization. (Three of the fifteen were subsequently ordered rehired with back pay.)

It was quite early in Hoving's regime that a staff member renamed the museum "Tavern in the Red," a pun on the Tavern on the Green across the park. Unless there is an independent audit someday, it will probably never be possible to chart the precise course of the deficit, since accounting procedures were changed from year to year and the sketchy annual reports fail to disclose the confusing shifts of money from one fund to another. There is no doubt, however, that the deficit was growing inexorably, despite successive increases in the city subsidy, successive cutbacks in museum hours and services and, most deplorably, the introduction of "voluntary donations" for admission.

Even before these were imposed on the public — the "suggested" rate for adults is $1.50 — attendance at the museum had fallen noticeably. Asked by the *Christian Science Monitor* how come, Hoving said he didn't know: "Certain things are way up, and certain things down." Later, when it transpired that attendance was one-third below the annual rate in Rorimer's time, Hoving replied that in those days the count was inflated. (The Hoving counterpunch technique would become familiar: the unpleasant figures were fake, the paintings were fake, the news reports were fake.)

The director put the blame for what he would call "the most severe financial crisis" in the museum's history on the 1969–70 recession and on inflation. Other museums were hurting, too, although it is doubtful that any other *subsidized* institution was spending a million and a half dollars a year or more above its operating revenues, and so being forced to dip deeply into its endowment.

Staff members put the blame on what they described as extravagance: for example, hiring high-salaried and hardnosed if inexperienced young executives; redecorating the cloakroom ceilings in gold leaf, then painting them over; redoing the façade at a cost of $2.2 million (to the violent objection of outside architects and aesthetes, who were barely able to save the great inner stairway from demolition); borrowing from capital funds to finance the construction of the Lehman Pavilion (during the battle, the public had been led to believe that the Lehman estate would pay for the building); and the confection of a $15,000 papier-mâché birthday cake which turned out to be in such poor taste that it was destroyed unseen.

The birthday in question was the 100th anniversary of the Metropolitan Museum, which was founded in 1870. Originally planned as a reasonably modest affair, it was expanded by Hoving into an eighteen-month extravaganza that occupied one hundred persons full time and cost millions, although no accounting was ever made public. It featured no fewer than eighty parties, offering caviar, pheasant pie and orchids; some of them held in the museum, at some loss to the draperies, and some outside, with old silver borrowed from the collections. The festivities included the camp-society bash of the decade (to be recounted in Chapter X). But the costliest event of all, in the broader sense, was beyond question the precentennial show called *Harlem on My Mind*.

This was 1969, the heyday of Radical Chic, when *Vogue* described the Republican Hoving as "the successful Establishment radical . . . a model for others to follow." If the ghetto would not come to the museum, the museum would go to the ghetto.

By golly, the ghetto would come to the museum as well! *Harlem on My Mind* would be the big sendoff, showing what black artists could do. Hoving was dissuaded, it is said, from painting galleries brown and black and from having the museum cafeteria serve soul food for the duration. Also, he soon abandoned the plan to hang work by black artists and replaced it with a photographically illustrated exhibition of Harlem life, mounted by a white man. Black artists picketed the opening with signs reading TRICKY TOM IS AT IT AGAIN and ART SHOW OR NO SHOW.

This was not irreparable; Hoving got a foundation grant and hired the picket leader to survey what the museum could do to promote the arts in the ghetto (a program that never came to anything). What did the heavy damage was the catalogue. Hoving wrote the lyrical preface in which he recounted what Harlem meant to him as a child on Park Avenue: "Times change, bodies change, minds change. When I grew up in New York, and when I was a boy of eight, nine, ten, eleven, twelve, there was a Harlem. And Harlem was with me and my family — a wonderful maid of sunny disposition and a thin, sour chauffeur who drove me to school in moody silence." (Barbara Goldsmith in *New York* magazine quoted his sister, Petrea, as exclaiming: "What does he mean? We never had a Negro maid or a chauffeur.")

This was followed by an essay by a black girl, which included the passage: "Behind every hurdle that the Afro-American has yet to jump stands the Jew, who has already cleared it . . . The already badly exploited Black, further exploited by the Jews . . . may find that anti-Jewish sentiments place them, for once, within a majority. Thus our contempt for the Jew makes us feel more completely American in sharing a national prejudice."

It developed that this passage had been lifted from a book by Daniel P. Moynihan and Nathan Glazer, and the quotation marks had allegedly been deleted by the producer of the show, himself Jewish. But it could hardly have been worse timed, coming in the wake of a New York school strike that pitted black parents against Jewish teachers. Jews picketed the Met, and rabbis read a sermon of grief and reproach in the city's synagogues. Even Mayor Lindsay publicly deplored the catalogue, and somebody introduced a bill to cancel the museum's subsidy. The catalogue was withdrawn with an apology by Hoving. But by then the offending passage had done its damage.

There was wide speculation that Hoving would get the ax at the next board meeting. What happened in fact was that Hoving turned up in great form and enchanted the trustees with a preview of his Master Plan and the goodies to come in the centennial proper. There was no question of dismissing him. However, Hoving himself hinted to Ms Goldsmith that he was thinking about laying down the burden: "I'll stay until after the Centennial. But all I can do will be done in five or six years. I think that term of office is right for a place like this. Six years and you can really accomplish something, but beyond that, it gets to be a kind of sinecure . . . Besides, I'm wearing out."

In an interview in early 1973, six and one-half years after his return to the Met, Hoving struck precisely the same note of weary willingness to turn over the helm to younger and fresher hands. (See Chapter XVII.) During the six-year period, he had given the trustees many another occasion to prove their devotion under trial. They never failed.

CHAPTER 6

Refining the Collections

> When I learned the other day that the National Gallery
> had bought that Leonardo for six million dollars, I
> couldn't sleep all night. We should have reached for
> it . . . If I live to the year 2,000, before I die there will
> be a painting sold for twenty-five million — well, a work
> of art, not necessarily a painting.
>
> — Thomas Hoving to John McPhee

When the Metropolitan Museum's great rival in Washington bought Leonardo da Vinci's *Ginevra de' Benci* from the Duke of Liechtenstein at the highest price ever paid for a painting, Ted Rousseau characteristically shrugged it off. He had long ago advised that the portrait was not worth the price, since it was scarcely in the class of the Mona Lisa. But Hoving by his own account spent a night tossing with remorse that he had not obtained the treasure for the Met. He finally obtained a small revenge.

On November 27, 1970, a portrait by Velázquez of his mulatto assistant, Juan de Pareja, went on sale at Christie's in London. The contest was fast and dramatic. Soon only two bidders were left, the dealers Alec Wildenstein and Geoffrey Agnew, the second of whom was representing the National Gallery. At the end, Agnew fell silent, and Wildenstein got the portrait for the highest price ever paid at a picture auction: $5,544,000. Wildenstein said, "It's a painting my great-grandfather Nathan wanted eighty years ago"; the gallery would keep it in inventory.

The following May, in a front-page story in *The New York Times*, Hoving and Met President Dillon disclosed that the Wildenstein gallery actually had bought the Velázquez for the Met. "The Museum is indebted to Wildenstein for its important assistance in the acquisition of this great picture and for its generosity in doing so at no cost to the Museum," they said.

How the Met repaid its moral obligation is a secret between the museum and Wildenstein, its chief supplier of old masters in recent decades. Another mystery never satisfactorily explained is the passage of more than five months between the sale at Christie's and the triumphant announcement in New York. Hoving told questioners that discretion was dictated by the need to obtain an export permit from Britain, but it hardly seems likely that the British would rather see the Velázquez go to a *private* collector abroad than to a great American museum.

One fact that had not been published when these lines were written is that, except for Dillon, *the trustees did not know that they had bought a Velázquez!* This was a violation of at least the spirit of the museum bylaws and a far cry from policy as carried on through the Rorimer regime; the purchase of the Rembrandt *Aristotle* was debated by the board for weeks before the auction. Retroactive approval was an innovation of the Hoving regime.

Echoing Hoving's new philosophy, Dillon declared: "As I've said publicly a number of times over the past year, our focus has changed from buying objects on a broad scale to the more difficult, but in the long run far more rewarding, tasks of concentrating the Museum's purchase funds, and waiting patiently for the rare and momentous occasion when an extraordinary work of art becomes available."

Dillon said the Velázquez had been bought with funds restricted to the purchase of art and "a few special gifts from friends of the Museum intended solely for this purpose." This was meant to allay murmurs of protest about the huge outlay at a time when the museum was running more than a million dollars a year in the red, imposing new admission charges and continually prying increases in its subsidy from the city.

There remained the fact that the trustees of two great American museums, using funds that, through tax deductions, would eventually come largely from the public purse, had bid up the price of a painting by millions of dollars above its estimated value.

The *Times* in an editorial said the price of a masterpiece was irrelevant to the city's mundane needs, and New York was lucky to have it. However, the editorial writer was doubtless unaware that there were at least five known versions of the *Juan de Pareja*, and one of them was hanging uptown at the Hispanic Society's museum. That one is attributed to the brush of Juan de Pareja himself; there are those who say that the Met's *Juan de Pareja* is a self-portrait, too, and others who say that although it is by Velázquez, it is not one of his very best. But a majority of experts think it is the master's own, and a fine one. Those are questions for the experts. It would be amusing, however, to switch the two portraits and see whether the public, gazing at the Hispanic Society's *Juan de Pareja* and thinking it to have been acquired for $5,544,000, would be any less thrilled.

Dillon's statement was misleading in one important respect. He had clearly implied that the Velázquez had been paid for. But a footnote to the annual report for the 1971–72 fiscal year revealed that an endowment fund was being reimbursed $133,000 a year for fifteen years in connection with a purchase. It transpired that most of the money had been borrowed from the Fletcher Fund, a half-century-old endowment, to pay for the Velázquez.

The same annual report, not coincidentally, showed that $2,106,893 had been transferred from endowment funds to pay for operations. Admissions were down 8 per cent and memberships down 27 per cent (reflecting an increase in dues). Despite a city contribution of $2,414,499 toward operating expenses (in addition to maintenance), the deficit had grown to $1,538,850. "Accordingly," said the treasurer, "with the full support of the Board of Trustees, a determined Budget Committee made up of the Director and his immediate staff took steps to reduce operating expenses for the 1973 fiscal year 10 percent below 1972." There followed a list of drastic cuts in services and staff.

At a staff meeting, one of those slated for the ax suggested that Hoving and his aides take pay cuts instead. "I will not," Hoving replied.

"There is no such thing as participatory budgetry," he told them.

What this meant in human terms was exemplified by Janine Borriau, a young Egyptologist whom Hoving had hired away from a job at the Ashmolean at Oxford with a glowing letter promising a happy career. She got her layoff notice, along with sixty-two others, after nine months. Jobs in Egyptology are scarce; at this writing, she has still not found a new post. (In early 1973, a memorandum by Dillon showed that authorized staff was again as large as before the 1972 layoffs.)

I asked a dealer wise in the ways of the art-buying rich why the trustees hadn't dug into their own pockets for the paltry few million needed to pay for their museum's new administration and acquisitions, not to mention their eighty lavish parties. Their combined wealth is incalculable and their generosity undeniable; several of the trustees have given very substantial sums without publicity. But unlike the Met, the dealer explained, as a class capitalists prefer to spend income rather than capital. The Internal Revenue

Code has created a pattern to their generosity: in a year of rising income, they climb into higher tax brackets, and, with Uncle Sam bearing a correspondingly larger share of the burden, their gifts rise accordingly. The years 1969–71 were recession years, and tax counselors advised their clients to defer their generosity.

It is curious to note the enthusiasm with which the Met entered into the spirit of tax avoidance. Dillon and Hoving said in their last annual report that 90 per cent of museum visitors "consider their contribution adequately repaid by their visit," but signs over the admissions booths told the public that the "donations" were tax deductible. The same approach is taken with membership fees, although they include subscriptions and other privileges. Getting full value for your money is a fairly questionable interpretation of a charitable donation under the tax code.

According to a curator, the museum in 1972 coöperated with an enormously wealthy trustee in what appeared to be a highly ingenious device to avoid a small tax bite. The trustee *gave* an anonymous cash donation to the Met, and his wife *sold* it two antiques at a price equal to the donation. Thus the couple got their money back but were out two antiques. Why not give the antiques outright? Well for one thing, as a tax authority explained, the value of the objects in that case would have to be appraised by independent experts. For another, the couple might use the "sale" to shore up their claim to be in the art business, and thus deduct their considerable expenses incurred in collection of art; they had lost just such a claim in a drawn-out suit with the government some years ago.

This is far from the only way that trustees benefit from their trusteeship. The couple in question — who, be it said, have given generously to the Met — also employed a curator to advise them and catalogue their collection, and they lend much of it to the museum, where its display enhances its value. But that is another story . . .*

The passion to acquire new works of great price at a time when the Met was in grave financial distress caused Hoving and Dillon to take another look at the museum's own incalculable store of treasures. This brought about a revolution in disposal policy.

Other directors had cleaned out storerooms of stuff regarded as inconsequential. Even so, they had made mistakes, as when Director Edward Robinson in the twenties sold part of the Cesnola collection of antiquities from Cyprus as redundant. It is recalled that two out of three look-alike stone heads were sold; they turned out to belong to a three-headed monster. The Cesnola sale is now deplored by scholars, who also regret the sale, ordered by Director Francis Henry Taylor in the fifties, of many thousands of minor Egyptian artifacts. Researchers who later wanted to apply new technology to the study of pots and their contents, as well as of other objects from the Met's diggings, were dismayed to learn that they had been dispersed.

It has always been considered that a great museum is a research institution as well as a showcase. At the time of his appointment as director in 1967, Hoving told John McPhee of *The New Yorker*: "The notion that we only collect masterpieces is false . . . we also collect backup

---

* Well, let's tell just one more. Allen Funt, the "Candid Camera" producer, decided to sell his collection of thirty-five paintings by the nearly forgotten Victorian academician Sir Lawrence Alma-Tadema. He got the Met to show the pictures in the spring of 1973, with a catalogue financed by Funt and written by Curator Fahy. After the show, Funt shipped the paintings and catalogue to Sotheby's for auction, with the museum's imprimatur a major selling point. Meanwhile, incidentally, the Met lent Funt an unknown number of French masters to cover the bare spaces on his walls.

material." Five years later, Hoving wrote in the *Times* that "the Metropolitan is not a Library of Congress of works of art . . . the business of a great art museum is quality, not numbers."

At the time of that writing, Hoving was secretly negotiating the sale of, among other things, two of the museum's most valuable paintings and irreplaceable collections of ancient coins.

CHAPTER 7

The Selling of the Met

> Decisions on how, when and where to sell require great knowledge, experience and intuition. Most knowledgeable persons agree that the museum is very well qualified to make such decisions and has been making them successfully for decades.
>
> — Thomas Hoving in a letter to the *Times*,
> October 31, 1972

In January 1972, a strange rumor began circulating along Madison Avenue, the capital of the American art market. The Metropolitan Museum, it was whispered, was peddling a lot of important French paintings. The names stirred disbelief: Picasso's *Woman in White;* Manet's *Portrait of George Moore* and *Boy with a Sword;* the historic Cézanne *Colline des Pauvres;* a Gauguin, and so on.

Incredible. But like the girl in the limerick, Eugene V. Thaw and John Rewald woke up to find it was perfectly true. Thaw, who was then president of the Art Dealers Association, and Rewald, an internationally known authority on the Impressionists, had heard the rumor at dinner parties. On visiting the Met to appraise some lesser pictures in the basement storerooms, Thaw put the question bluntly to young Everett Fahy, the curator of European paintings. According to Thaw, Fahy replied: "Yes, it's true. I'm trying to stop it."

Rewald, too, decided to try to stop it. He wrote an article recalling past follies of American museums that had sold in haste and repented at leisure, and revealing that the Met was now engaged in a similar adventure. Four magazines rejected it before it finally appeared in *Art in America* nearly a year later. But the paintings would long since have vanished into the international art market had Rewald waited till then to act. Instead, he and Thaw picked up Ralph J. Colin, counsel to the Art Dealers Association, and the three went calling on John Canaday, the art critic of *The New York Times*.

Grace Glueck, the cultural news reporter, phoned Hoving at Canaday's suggestion. The director denied the rumors but acknowledged that some sales were being considered and, as he put it later, "If and when the Board did come to a final decision, the museum would make an announcement." Meanwhile, however, it was learned that the paintings had already been, in the barbarous museum jargon, "de-accessioned" — that is, removed from the registry of the Met's collections — and that preparations for their sale at auction were well advanced. It was, however, Hoving's word against Ms Glueck's knowledge, based on sources that could not be revealed. Under the circumstances, it was felt, the story was not quite fit to print in the news columns of the *Times*. Canaday thereupon decided to tell it in his Sunday column, where he had full liberty to express opinions.

The piece appeared on February 27, 1972, a date that surely will stand out in the history of the Met's second century. In retrospect, it seems restrained. Under the headline "Very Quiet and Very Dangerous," Canaday broke the story of the planned sales as "rumors." He recalled similar deals by other museums and conceded that they were perfectly legal. "But are these sales always ethical?" he asked, replying, "More likely, shortsighted."

Canaday recalled that the Chicago Art Institute had sold

a lot of Monets in 1944 for less than it would pay for one of them today, that the Minneapolis Institute of Arts had unloaded a treasure of old masters for a song, that the Guggenheim would be glad to have back the ninety-seven Kandinskys it had sold.

He pointed out that when art is given to museums the donors deduct its value from their income for tax purposes, so that in effect the taxpaying public helps pay for the gifts; further, he added, if this art is then sold and ultimately donated to another museum, the taxpayers can find themselves paying over and over for the same picture. They might put in question the very principle of tax deductions on art, he warned.

"In effect the public buys the work," Canaday concluded. "By any ethical standard, the pubic owns them. When such works are sold, the seller-museum violates a fiduciary trust."

The *Times* more than courteously pulled back a page of the next Sunday art section as it was going to press and yanked an article to permit Hoving to reply. His piece, headed "Very Inaccurate and Very Dangerous," was as violent an attack on a journalist as ever to appear in his own paper. The Canaday piece, he said, was "99 per cent inaccurate" and "grossly incorrect." As a sample of its inaccuracy, Hoving said, the Manet portrait of George Moore in question was "not the glorious Havemeyer pastel vibrant with life and wit that came to the museum in 1929 but an unfinished painting of Moore that came to the Metropolitan in 1955." (The reader would do well to parse the foregoing sentence twice: it at once confirms what Hoving was denying — that the museum was contemplating the sale of a Manet portrait — and clobbers Canaday for an inconsequential error of detail, the only one in his article. The museum indeed owned — and thanks to Canaday still does — two Manet portraits of George Moore. In checking his list, Canaday innocently assumed the Met was selling the pastel; the "unfinished" oil, as Thaw commented later with indignation, is regarded as one of Manet's most beautiful paintings.)

"In the past 20 years," Hoving wrote, "I would say that the museum has disposed of 15,000 works of art." (Most of them were scarabs, beads and pottery from the museum's once-major Egyptian digs, sold through the Met bookstore. Relatively few art objects of price had been sold before the Hoving era.) "The process has been quite open," Hoving said, and its purpose was, in a phrase he would repeat again and again, "to upgrade and refine the quality of the collections." He concluded: "The sad thing about Mr. Canaday's article is not its inaccuracy or its surprising lack of recognition of a well established museum practice, but that it implies strongly that the Metropolitan has been and is equivocal, clandestine and even possibly unethical in an activity that it has been pursuing responsibly and well for decades."

One of the curious aspects of this brief flap is that at least ten trustees of the Met presumably knew that Canaday had been telling the truth. They were the members of the Acquisitions Committee, formerly and more prosaically called the Purchasing Committee. (There is no disposal committee, since it had never been contemplated that the museum needed one. The function is vested in the Acquisitions Committee.) It was headed by the banker-statesman C. Douglas Dillon, president of the Met, and included Hoving and Arthur Ochs Sulzberger, publisher of the *Times*. Months earlier, they had authorized the disposal of the paintings in question, as confirmed by photocopies of museum records that I obtained long afterward. But trustee meetings under the Dillon-Hoving regime had become like directors' meetings of many corporations — quite brief and perfunctory; it may be that the sale of these masterpieces had scarcely registered in their minds.

When Canaday's article appeared, the Met was already negotiating to sell to the Museum of Modern Art the magnificent Picasso *Woman in White,* and Sotheby Parke Bernet was already preparing a catalogue for the auction of other paintings that he had mentioned. But if the trustees were not surprised at the news, the heirs of some donors were. Two daughters of the late Sam Lewisohn, a member of the family of bankers and connoisseurs that included the Lehmans, told museum officials that they were shocked to learn that their father's Gauguin and Renoir were being put on the market. They said remaining masterpieces in their hands would never be left to the museum if that happened.

Robert S. Pirie of Boston had a curious experience. His mother, the late Mrs. Ralph J. Hines, had given the Met a number of valuable paintings in the mid fifties. Upon learning that the museum was now in the selling game, he telephoned a friend at the museum to say that, should any of his mother's pictures be sold, he'd like to have a chance to bid on it. The friend said yes, the Manet *George Moore* — Mrs. Hines's donation, not the Havemeyer one — was indeed being considered for disposal, but he set a market value on it that caused Pirie to bow out. Idly, the Bostonian asked if there was any chance the Met would sell his mother's El Greco, *St. Catherine of Alexandria.* His informant replied that this was not under consideration. Weeks later, Pirie was browsing in a publication of Sotheby, the London auction house, and was startled to see the *St. Catherine* there; it had been sold for $120,000 in an important auction of old masters from various collections on June 24, 1970.

Pirie called his friend back; this time he was told that the picture had been sold privately in 1965, when the museum discovered that it was not by El Greco. Curiously, however, it was presented as a genuine El Greco in Sotheby's catalogue, with the Met listed as the last of six distinguished owners, its authenticity buttressed by no fewer than nine references in the El Greco literature. The last authority cited, Professor H. E. Wethey of the University of Michigan, told me later that though he didn't consider the *St. Catherine* an *important* El Greco (as witness the price of $120,000 paid for it), he did not doubt its authenticity (while granting that El Greco's assistants might have worked on it as well). The museum several times promised to dig out the answers to my questions: to whom had it sold the El Greco, for how much, and why? I never got them.

The excuse from the museum public relations office was that any further information on past deals was now reserved for a forthcoming "white paper" designed to rebut my investigative reports. But Hoving himself indicated to *New York* magazine that it would be hard to figure what the Met had received for the El Greco. Breaking his own embargo on the story, he said: "In 1965, to get a Jacques-Louis David and four panels by Lorenzo Monaco, we traded to Wildenstein & Company three Renoirs, four Monets, an El Greco and a Rouault, plus giving them $625,000 in cash." Try untangling that one!

By the time Pirie asked about his mother's El Greco, a pattern had been established that recalls the old line "I never borrowed your pot, and besides, it was broken." Confronted with the secret and curious disposal of a painting, the Met would at first deny it, then say the picture was suspicious, bad or an outright fake. This made it look as though the museum officials had engaged in a rather sharp practice — the sale of paintings under false or misleading attributions — while permitting the dealer-buyers to *resell* them bearing not only the original attribution but also the imprimatur of the Metropolitan Museum. It may be, however, that in the milieu of the trustees it is considered preferable to look like a sharp operator than to look like a sucker.

The paintings mentioned by Canaday were hastily withdrawn from the market and quietly "re-accessioned." The collection was now, it appeared, whole again. In one respect, in fact, it was better than ever. In a rare act of insubordination, Curator Fahy had sent the Cézanne to be cleaned, against the wishes of his superiors. The painting was the first Cézanne to be bought by an American museum; the Met had acquired it when it was exhibited at the famous Armory Show of 1913. Often loaned to other museums, it was in deplorable condition. It returned from the cleaning in all its glory, and there was no further question of selling it.

Hoving had promised that if any decision was taken to sell any art, a public announcement would be made. Since there was none for the next six months, it was generally assumed that the affair of the de-accessionings was closed. It was — in the sense that no word appeared in the press. But Eugene Thaw, the dealer, vividly recalls a lunch with Fahy at the Regency Hotel in late spring. He says the young curator arrived pale and evidently under great distress and told him: "It's worse than you know. I've just been through a grilling. They were trying to make me sign something."

Fahy would not say what it was he had been asked to sign in that now-famous session with Hoving, Rousseau and the museum's secretary, Ashton Hawkins. He refused to sign, he said, but the act appeared to exhaust his courage; from then on, he would answer no questions about the disposal of pictures in his charge.

Thaw, however, could guess the general nature of what was being demanded of Fahy — his approval of an important sale.

Hoving himself had helped draft the ethical guidelines of the Association of Art Museum Directors, which said:

DISPOSALS

29. The disposal of a work of art from a museum's collection requires particularly rigid examination because such an action is usually irrevocable. When the retention of all material entering a collection can be justified, disposal on grounds of taste is problematical and should be exercised with great caution. Any disposal should be related to a broad policy rather than to the exigencies of the moment.

30. Should such a disposal be undertaken, full justification of the action should be provided to the Board by the Director and the responsible Curator; final action should rest with the Board. It is advisable that the voting procedure in reaching such a decision be at least as rigorous as that for acquisitions.*

In September 1972, in line with its promise to announce any new dispositions, the Met disclosed three forthcoming sales at auction, through Sotheby of London and its New York subsidiary, Parke Bernet. One involved the bulk of the museum's coin collections (actually, the deal had been made the preceding winter, but of that, more later); the second involved a dozen French Impressionists; and the third would comprise 123 old masters (eventually there

---

* The guidelines also say that "no work should be accepted with an attribution or circumstances of exhibition guaranteed in perpetuity." Such as those, for example, that had been guaranteed by Hoving for the Lehman and Rockefeller collections.

were 146, all relatively minor paintings). The French pictures included an Odilon Redon, a Monet, a Sisley, a Degas, a Toulouse-Lautrec, two Boudins and two Renoirs. (One was withdrawn suddenly from sale; the remaining eleven fetched $574,500, about twice what Parke Bernet had estimated.) "There are some pretty good pictures," Hoving allowed, "but they aren't important for the Metropolitan." There was some grumbling. The very day this news appeared, however, it was blotted out by a new sensation.

Norton Simon, the tycoon collector, confided to a dealer that in his hotel room in London he had been shown a van Gogh, *The Olive Pickers,* which had belonged to the Met but was being offered him by Frank Lloyd of the Marlborough galleries. (The asking price, I later learned, was $1,500,000.) Simon was told that the Met had also sold Lloyd *Tropics,* popularly called "Monkeys in the Jungle," by Douanier Rousseau. (No kin to the Met's chief curator; the quip in the museum was "They sold the wrong Rousseau!")

When this report reached Canaday at the *Times,* he called Hoving, who at first denied, then confirmed it. The director expressed surprise at the rumors that it had been offered for resale: "My feeling is that it's not possible," he said. He indicated that he had been approached six months earlier by a private collector with a generous offer to buy the two paintings. This had been accepted gratefully, and the proceeds had been applied to the upgrading of the collections — notably the Velázquez *Juan de Pareja* and the Annibale Carracci *Coronation of the Virgin.* Hoving would not say who the collector was, nor how much he had paid. But Canaday had heard that it was Giovanni Agnelli, the president of Fiat and a financial backer of Lloyd's, and I later learned that the price of the two pictures was

$1,450,000,* which was less than Lloyd was asking for the van Gogh alone. (Still later, *Time*'s man in Tokyo, where Lloyd had opened a new branch, reported that the Rousseau had been sold to an industrialist from Osaka for $2,000,000.)

The Art Dealers Association was understandably upset, both on moral and on financial grounds: if museums were to unload holdings in a big way, that would unsettle the market; and if they were to keep on making private deals, many dealers would be left out. Some of the members had in fact made private deals of their own with the Met, it transpired, but none on the scale of the Marlborough's purchase. So under the name of Ralph J. Colin, general counsel of the dealer's association (and of Marlborough!), they issued a statement denouncing the sale of the van Gogh and the Rousseau as "a breach of public trust." If the Met must sell art, they said, it should do it in the open, explain its reasons, and give first preference to other museums as buyers and second preference to the open market, "so that the maximum proceeds are assured." They added that Fahy had not approved the sales in question, as required under the museum standards of ethics.

In reply, Hoving acknowledged that Marlborough was the only dealer consulted but said, "We couldn't have gotten a better price." He added that Fahy *had* "recommended the de-accessioning of the pictures," but the price to be received was the concern of the trustees alone. (Theodore Rousseau has told me that Fahy disagreed only

---

* Fahy had appraised the paintings at $1.6 million, and at least twice he had appealed to the trustees not to sell the Douanier Rousseau, which he described as "more than worthy" of the artist. Dillon, Hoving and Rousseau overruled him on the grounds that the Rousseau was inferior and that the price was generous in light of earlier auction levels and a Parke Bernet appraisal. Parke Bernet appraisals had been running far below auction prices actually realized.

about the price; Fahy's lips having been sealed, I could not determine whether he ever actually signed the recommendation alluded to by Hoving. His friends say he did not.)

As for the van Gogh and Rousseau, Hoving went on: "We have far better pictures in both areas by both artists. We decided to sell them to buy great things by masters who we simply don't have and will never be available again. We exchanged weak modern masters for strong old masters."

In Italy, where Fiat workers were clamoring for a pay raise, the communists made hay out of the report that Agnelli had just bought a couple of paintings worth well over $2,000,000. Frank Lloyd in New York retorted angrily that Agnelli had nothing to do with the purchase and that the *Times* had queered a resale of *Tropics* to the Italian. However, Theodore Rousseau admitted that Agnelli's name "might have come up" in the negotiations. Advised by Canaday of Marlborough's statement, Hoving said with a charming air of candor: "I was surprised the other day; today I'd expect anything."

Also surprised were some trustees and other insiders. They had been told that the two pictures had been sold to Agnelli, who in gratitude would build for the museum several "artmobiles." These are big museum vans like those used in Sweden to bring art to the hinterland. During the fight over the Lehman Pavilion, Hoving had promised the city that it would have such vehicles to serve the five boroughs. Nothing ever came of it.

Three days after his disclosure of the van Gogh–Rousseau sale, Canaday exploded another bomb. He revealed that the Met had given Marlborough a Modigliani, *Red Head*, and a Juan Gris, *Le Guéridon*, in exchange for a sculpture by the late David Smith and a painting, reportedly by Clyfford Still. Hoving brushed this off with the comment, "There will be mistakes in disposing, but they will not be as serious as mistakes in not getting."

By this time, the art world was astir and divided into two camps. By far the larger one, comprising a majority of collectors, scholars and museum-goers, was harshly critical of the Met. Several past donors declared publicly, and many more privately, that they would never give anything more; "I wonder," wrote Francis Steegmuller, "why any citizen should offer works of art to these arrogant institutions." Eight New York art historians wrote the *Times*, complaining that their letter to the Met had not been acknowledged and expressing distress that works of art, "after years in the public domain, should return to private hands or even leave this country permanently."

A few voices rose to Hoving's defense. His old friend Mayor Lindsay fell silent and remained so through the storms to come, but Hoving's successor as parks commissioner, August Heckscher, Jr., called him "extraordinarily brilliant, inventive and effective [and] completely within his rights."

Several museum directors, who had themselves often engaged in secret art dealing, saw the anti-Hoving furor as a threat to their freedom of action. Thomas Buechner, retired director of the Brooklyn Museum, wrote the *Times:*

"Museums do not exist to provide warehousing in perpetuity. To require such institutions to sell publicly while everyone else sells privately would be a decided disadvantage . . . It might eliminate buyers who value their privacy, permit the formation of cartels, alienate proved channels of disposal . . . and undermine confidence in the museum through misunderstanding, as apparently it has in this instance."

(Soon afterward, Buechner himself became the victim of

a similar misunderstanding. The Harvard art historian Seymour Slive revealed that Buechner had secretly sold in 1967 a major work by Frans Hals, which he called one of the best in the country. Buechner, now president of Steuben Glass, a subsidiary of Arthur Houghton's Corning, would not reveal whether or not he had consulted experts, but said he didn't think much of the picture. It reportedly went to Wildenstein for $250,000; now said to be owned by a Swiss collector, it is thought to be worth more than $1 million.)

Mitchell Wilder of the Amon Carter Museum in Fort Worth, Texas, president of the Association of Art Museum Directors, told me: "You people get yourselves awfully excited. This is an internal matter. I'm sure the Met does things in what they consider the best interests of the institution."

This outlook was not unanimous, however, and it became less so as museums across the country met growing uneasiness among donors. Sherman Lee of the Cleveland Museum and J. Carter Brown of the National Gallery both expressed reservations about the way the Met had handled its disposals. But when the issue was raised before the ethics committee of the museum directors, it was shelved.

Douglas Dillon, president of the Met, came loyally to Hoving's defense. In a guest article in the *Times* headed "The Metropolitan Sets the Record Straight," he again explained the process of selling to refine and upgrade the collections, and revealed that

> In the light of the current debate, the board has reaffirmed and clarified its policy that no work of art valued by the curator at $10,000 or over will be disposed of until it has been ascertained that there is no objection from the donor, or that there has been a reasonable inquiry among available heirs of the donor or testator, or their available represen-

tatives, who have expressed no objection to such sale or
disposal . . . This work of de-accessioning and disposal
is not done capriciously. An elaborate system of checks,
balances and reviews is in force, and we often seek outside,
expert opinions . . . the Acquisitions Committee of the
Board of Trustees studies, evaluates and votes on each work
of art recommended for disposal . . . These procedures
were carefully followed in all the cases which have been the
subject of recent press comment. It is worthy of note that
they are in full accord with the guidelines for such action
recently promulgated by the Ethics and Practices Committee
of the Association of Art Museum Directors . . . The
Acquisitions Committee is a highly responsible group of
individuals, many of whom have had considerable personal
experience in the art market.

Dillon is a tall, white-haired, usually soft-spoken man,
who could be a Hollywood typecast for the role of distinguished diplomat, banker or secretary of the treasury —
each of which, of course, he has been. It is difficult to
believe that he gave any serious attention to this article
before it was published.* One would prefer to believe that,
as staff members assert, this Dillon statement like others
was drafted by Ashton Hawkins, the hard-nosed young
secretary of the Met, and read to Dillon on the phone. The
president may have been distracted when he heard it or,
perhaps, since he was on his Florida estate much of the
time, he was out of touch with events. None of the foregoing passages could withstand close investigation.

---

* Dillon's public career has not been free of ambiguity, however. When
he, a Republican banker, agreed to become President Kennedy's secretary of the treasury, there were some mutterings in the Club about
treason. However, the administration soon abandoned the tax reform
program that had frightened Wall Street and began a program of tax
incentives and financial hocus-pocus that finally led to the monetary
crises of recent years. The subject is too complex for a footnote, but
it is curious that a conservative banker could so easily be sold on deficit
spending — by a government or by a museum.

Following the Canaday exposé in late February 1972, the trustees did adopt new guidelines for art disposals; but according to one published account, never denied, they also authorized Dillon and Hoving to execute major deals on their own signatures. The trustees also ordered that heirs be consulted on any future sales — which incidentally tore a small hole in the argument that art would be sold only because it was not needed; a prior condition henceforth was that such works be free of family embarrassments. (This, as Mrs. Lee Seldes has pointed out, might have been a bit ticklish with regard to the van Gogh *Olive Pickers*. It had once belonged to the late Vincent Astor, two of whose successive wives, Mrs. Brooke Astor and Mrs. Minnie Fosburgh, now sat on the Acquisitions Committee.)

Another condition was that the sales raise large sums of money; and the scraps from the storerooms would not do. Having had to re-accession the lot of French masters they had originally chosen, the Hoving team set out to find replacements. Rousseau was assigned to persuade the heirs. He admitted later, with a self-depreciating smile, that he had been a little dilatory; two or three families were called only hours before the sale at Sotheby Parke Bernet, and one of them balked, making it necessary to remove one of the twelve, a Boudin, from under the auctioneer's hammer.

Another family of wealth and stature was persuaded to let the masterpiece given by Mother be sold privately, on the museum's plea that an extraordinary price had been obtained for it — and on the promise that the proceeds would be used to buy art of the kind Mother had collected, the great French masters of the late nineteenth century. Further, the family would have a veto over what was bought in her name.

My later investigations for the *Times* revealed that the price obtained for Mother's painting was hardly generous, and that the proceeds had been applied to help pay for

Hoving's Velázquez and Carracci. The family then considered making a public protest but decided against it, presumably for the same reason that Mrs. Astor wouldn't vote against Charlie Wrightsman: social relations within the Club could be upset. Ultimately, the family was told that it still had a credit with the museum for the purchase of post-Impressionists in Mother's name.

Living heirs turned out to be a bloody nuisance. So there was welcome news indeed in a memorandum for Secretary Hawkins. On inquiry, it said, he had confirmed that Adelaide was the last of the de Groots.

CHAPTER 8

Adelaide

> The only questions that really matter ultimately in life
> are moral ones.
>
> — Thomas Hoving, in his 1968 commencement address
> at Bennington College

An artist who had married money once confided to me that
it was a hard way to make a dollar. In that sense, the
Metropolitan Museum may be said to have fairly earned the
fortune it got from Adelaide Milton de Groot. It is perhaps a delicate moral question. In any case, the wooing,
winning and betrayal of Adelaide are a classic of the genre.

She was a personnage straight from the pages of Henry
James. Born in New York in 1876 of distinguished Dutch
and Yankee forebears, she could recall the days when her
father's sailing ships, home from the China trade, poked
their bowsprits over South Street. Like other New York
aristocrats of her day, she spoke with a broad "A," and with
a refined "oi" in words like "church." She attended Miss
Bracket's School and the Art Students League, and until
she was twenty-five she was never permitted to go out
without a governess or, later, a lady companion. The
youngest of five daughters, she is said by those who knew
her to have been a bit spoiled, and to have grown into a
strong-willed, imperious woman.

The de Groots moved to Nice when she was fifteen, and
from the Gay Nineties to the outbreak of World War

I — that is, in the Henry James years — they lived in the social whirl of the international set on the Riviera. Every day, as she recalled it, there was a tea here, a dinner there, a ball somewhere else, with no time to do anything but change gowns. One of the girls married a Count d'Aspremont ("He was a great catch," Miss de Groot once told an interviewer. "We didn't know he took dope"), but the couple and their daughter died a few years later. The other sisters never wed.

Although, as she related, she had been "brought up to be a society woman, not a professional," Miss de Groot moved to Paris after the First World War and took up painting and collecting. Curiously, she does not seem to have penetrated the whirl of genius and hangers-on centered on such figures as Gertrude Stein, Picasso, Joyce and Hemingway. Except for the company of a few attentive art dealers, her life when away from the easel consisted chiefly of playing bridge with ladies of the large colony of wealthy Americans in Paris. This schizoid pattern deepened when she went home for good in 1933, along with most of that American colony after the crash and the devaluation of the dollar had made living in Paris less attractive. At New York meetings of the Colonial Dames and the Daughters of Holland Dames, she was every inch the lady in proper, albeit stout, dresses and white gloves. However, she lived in a one-room flat on the unfashionable *West* Side (as she had lived in the humble Bastille quarter of Paris), kept no servant and took what passed for meals from tins, sometimes boiling an egg in a can on a tiny stove. To friends who expostulated, she replied, "That's how artists live."

Her family antiques and her large collection of paintings she lent to museums in New York and Connecticut, where her mother's family came from. She promised them all that they could keep these things when she died. There ensued, over more than two decades, an assiduous courtship of the aging spinster by a covey of museum directors and curators. By all accounts, she made the most of it. When she wanted to revisit those of her pictures hanging at the Met, for example, she would telephone ahead and be met at the door by the director or the handsome young Ted Rousseau and an underling or two, with a wheelchair in the later years, and be taken on a guided tour. She was touched when Rorimer appeared at her door one Thanksgiving Day with a turkey dinner in a basket and sat with her while she ate it. (The tale nowadays is told with a snicker, but underneath his sometimes authoritarian manner, Rorimer was a shy and sentimental man, and his motive here was undoubtedly one of pure kindness to a lonely woman.) Best of all was the respect that the Met paid to Miss de Groot's connoisseurship. In 1958, Rousseau helped mount a charity show, *Masterpieces from the Adelaide Milton de Groot Collection*, at the Perls Galleries. He wrote a glowing preface to the catalogue, which appeared alongside a reproduction of Modigliani's *Red Head* — the very one he later denounced. It is worth repeating here:

> The entire life of Adelaide Milton de Groot has been dominated by her interest in art. She has always been an active painter, from her early years in Nice until the present day. Her own creative efforts led her to the study of the old masters and an appreciation of her contemporaries, and inspired her to form a collection representing both the established traditions and the revolutionary movements of the twentieth century. Such a broad range is unusual among the collectors of our time. Exceptional also has been Miss de Groot's constant desire to share her collection in all its variety with the people who, like her, are enthusiastic about painting. For the last twenty years she has lent to American museums selections of her paintings, thus bringing to the

public an opportunity to enjoy them and learn from them. The present exhibition, which is only a fraction of the large group she has brought together, is one more example of her generous spirit. It presents to the New York public another remarkable aspect of Miss de Groot's personality—her astuteness and her far-sighted judgment in buying, long before they were fashionable, the works of painters who have since become the most highly regarded artists of our time. This is a collection formed by a cultivated taste, and it will surely delight all who have an opportunity to see it.

THEODORE ROUSSEAU, JR.
Curator of Paintings
The Metropolitan Museum of Art

The year following this gratification, Miss de Groot changed her will. Instead of dividing her treasures among a number of museums, as she had previously planned, she left everything, except for a few token bequests, to the Met: her collection of 213 works of art, the remaining paintings from her own hand, and the residue of her fortune, which came to nearly $1.5 million when she finally passsed on in 1967, at the age of ninety-one. Tragically, Rorimer had died the year before, so the fruits of his patient attendance went to the administration of Thomas P. F. Hoving.

Miss de Groot was a woman who knew what she wanted. She had dictated the terms of the bequest herself, and some of her strong personality emerges from the legal jargon. The clause of her will leaving her paintings to the Met read:

Without limiting in any way the absolute nature of this bequest, I request said Metropolitan Museum of Art not to sell any of said works of art, but to keep such of said works of art as it desires to retain for itself, and to give the balance to such one or more important Museums as said Metropolitan Museum of Art shall select, giving preference, first, to Museums situated in the Borough of Manhattan, City of New York, second, to Museums situated elsewhere in the State of New York, and third, to Museums situated in the State of Connecticut.

Long afterward, when I learned that the Met had sold at least fifty of the paintings and given none to any other museums, Rousseau told me he had himself suggested to Miss de Groot the phrase "Without limiting in any way the absolute nature of this bequest." This, he said, made her request "precatory," a legal term from the Latin word meaning "to pray." Thus, Miss de Groot was *praying*, rather than *ordering*, that the museum not sell her bequest. A lawyer who had studied the will told me this interpretation could be challenged in view of the emphatic nature of her request and the fact that a later clause of her will repeats it without the precatory phrase. "But who's going to sue?" the lawyer asked.

Who, again, would sue over Miss de Groot's money? Her fortune was in the care of the First National City Trust Company. It is worthy of note that Arthur Houghton, Jr., then president and now chairman of the Met, is also a director of National City and a member of its trust board, and Richard S. Perkins, a trustee of the Met who later signed a defense of what was done with Miss de Groot's money, was chief executive of the trust company when she changed her will and chairman of the executive committee of the bank when it turned the money over to the Met. It goes without saying that neither Houghton nor Perkins would knowingly be party to "hustling an old spinster for her money," as the foregoing lawyer described Operation Adelaide. But no junior officer of National City could be expected to be nosy about the execution of a trust agreement by a philanthropic institution run by such prestigious members of the Club.

With regard to her money, Miss de Groot's language was even more emphatic and binding than with regard to her paintings. She left her fortune to the Met

PROVIDED, HOWEVER, that said Metropolitan Museum shall first obligate itself in writing to expend the income from said principal, and, to the extent that said Metropolitan Museum may from time to time in its sole discretion deem it advisable, the said principal, for general archaeological (including not only ancient but mediaeval) investigation, excavation and research, preferably in Europe and Africa, or for any research which may appertain to the seventeenth century immigrants to New Amsterdam (New York City), or to what is now Brooklyn, New York, or to Stamford, Stratford, Monroe or Fairfield in the State of Connecticut, or for any research which may appertain to John Coggeshall, who was the first president of the independent colony of Rhode Island, and for the publication, at least once in every three years, of a book or pamphlet describing the work which has been done with this money since the last such book or pamphlet was published . . .

This time, there were no *ifs, ands* or precatory phrases, although Miss de Groot allowed that since, "at certain times (e.g., during widespread war), it may not be practicable to send out an expedition to do the more usual forms of archaeological research," the studies might be done among old documents in monasteries and such.

The settling of Adelaide de Groot's estate was completed in late 1970. The museum signed an obligation to carry out her wishes and the First National City Trust Company turned over the money and closed the account. Nearly $1.5 million vanished into the Met's dwindling capital funds . . . It was not until the following autumn, it appears, that anybody gave another thought to the obligation. Hoving's office then canvassed the curators to learn how much each department might be spending on research. At their meeting in November 1971, the trustees were advised that $212,320 had been assigned from the de Groot fund for archaeological work during the current fiscal year. The bill included $1200 in dues to scholarly organizations, $8000 in travel grants, mostly unspecified, and $22,870 to the conservation department for salaries of people who mend pottery and such.

The trustees were told that the Ancient Near East department devoted five sevenths of its budget to research, the Egyptian department one half and the Greek and Roman department five sevenths. By coincidence, each of these figures came to precisely $60,000, and the de Groot fund was duly so billed. A more detailed report in the folder given each trustee explained that the Near East department's research consisted primarily of the preparation of an exhibition of artifacts from an earlier dig in Iraq, and the Egyptian work comprised two studies (long since finished and already with the publishers), a picture book series, research connected with loan exhibitions and research on the erection of the Temple of Dendur. Archaeological work in Greece and Italy was now stymied, the trustees were told, because digs had "by now come under strict Government control," so the Greco-Roman department could make its best contribution by analyzing objects "now separated from their original site."*

In short, as Met staff members observed, the museum had billed Miss de Groot for expenditures it would have had to undertake even if she had not left it a dime. It was thus free to spend an equivalent sum as it pleased; in the jargon,

---

* This was not precisely what Miss de Groot meant by circumstances such as "widespread war." What "strict Government control" did mean was that the museum would be welcome to dig, but couldn't take away much of what it found. All it would get out of it was scholarship.

the museum had turned a restricted fund into unrestricted funds. An elderly trustee objected that this did not seem precisely what Miss de Groot had in mind. At the following meeting, in March 1972, President Dillon reported that General Counsel Herbert Brownell, the former United States attorney general, had found that the projects as outlined, "with a few minor changes," were "within the provisions of the de Groot Trust." The amount allowed had been trimmed by $250 to $212,070.

Approved.

A detail remained. Miss de Groot had instructed that a piece of research financed by her be published every three years. Warily, she had added: "Such book or pamphlet shall be a separate publication dealing solely with the work which has been accomplished through this fund, and it shall not be merely combined with, or incorporated as a part of, some other publication issued by said Museum." Secretary Hawkins, a lawyer by trade, asked general counsel whether a little footnote in the *Metropolitan Museum of Art Bulletin* would do the trick. Regretfully (we may assume), general counsel said no. When I inquired a year later, a spokesman told me that the Met hoped to get something published in Miss de Groot's name by 1975. That would be eight years after her death . . .

Miss de Groot *did* get her name in a museum book, however. This was the history commissioned by the Met and published in 1970 under the title *Merchants and Masterpieces.* The author, Calvin Tomkins, therein describes Miss de Groot as a "cross" that Rorimer had smilingly borne for many years. She "had spent forty years of her life in Europe, painting hideous landscapes and buying second-rate pictures by the important French artists of her day." She was eccentric in her life style, boiling eggs in empty orange juice cans to avoid buying a pot, and "threatened regularly to remove all her pictures and give them to another museum, a step that might have come as a relief to the Paintings Department . . ." But the "pilgrimages" of the curators to her flat "prevailed, however, and the museum eventually got the money."

Tomkins' book is on sale on the museum's main floor. If one considers that Miss de Groot's will was flouted, it may appear that the Met has added insult to injury. The Met did not *have* to court her, after all . . . Miss de Groot doubtless had an exaggerated view of her own talent, but her landscapes hardly deserve the epithet "hideous"; to the uninformed amateur, they seem agreeable. Tomkins' language is a reflection, rather, of what was being said in the administrative wing of the Met. When I was inquiring about the fate of Miss de Groot's paintings, Theodore Rousseau told me she had bought "a lot of junk." He described her Modigliani (the one in the 1958 catalogue alongside his eulogy) as a probable fake and her Douanier Rousseau, *Tropics*, which went to Japan, as very inferior Rousseau indeed. Cornelius Vermeule, then acting director of the Boston Museum of Fine Arts, scoffed: "If that Rousseau was so lousy, why did they send it to us in their *100 Masterpieces* show?"

Many of Miss de Groot's pictures *were* minor things — she had conceded that, when she prayed that the Met give them to other museums if it didn't want to keep them — but quite a few were very important indeed. Among these were her van Gogh self-portrait with the *Potato Peeler* on the reverse side (a prize on permanent exhibition) and the *Tropics*, which some experts regard as finer than the Rousseau that still hangs at the Met.

Poor Adelaide.

CHAPTER 9

Odalisque

> Max Friedländer, the great art historian, once said, "It may be an error to buy a work of art and discover that it is a fake, but it is a sin to call a fake something that is genuine."
>
> — Thomas Hoving to John McPhee

One day in January 1973, Edith Pearson was packing to move to a job at the Los Angeles County Museum of Art. A tall, slender and attractive young woman in Afro, she had resigned six months earlier as an assistant to the registrar at the Metropolitan Museum.

It had been a good job once, keeping track of the museum's treasures, but, she told me, "These last few years have been hell." Especially, there had been the tidal wave of de-accessionings. In fiscal 1970, as Ms Pearson remembered it, there had been about thirty objects so processed for disposal; the following year there were 1150.

"At one point," she said, "I had fourteen Monets on a list for de-accessioning. I don't know what the final decision was." In June 1972, when she quit in disgust, the catalogue and photo-record departments were hit by massive economy layoffs, but even before, Ms Pearson related, security procedures had been relaxed to the point that officials would take pictures over to Madison Avenue without signing them out.

"Our insurance underwriters would have had apoplexy," Ms Pearson said. "Somebody would phone from the entry and say 'Mister So-and-So is here from a gallery' — Wildenstein, or another — 'with a painting, and asks for a receipt.' We didn't know it was out of the building."

Art could also *join* the collections without her knowledge. When she was told to register the $5,544,000 Velázquez bought for the museum as a courtesy by Wildenstein, the order from upstairs lacked the usual information as to when it had been acquired and by whose donation.*

"There was always something cooking with Wildenstein," she said.

(Most of the old masters acquired by the Met in recent years seem to have come through Wildenstein. One of the most notable was *The Fortune Teller* by Georges de La Tour, whose date of acquisition is not entirely clear. The painting had been spotted by a man from the Louvre in a chateau in the Anjou, but the late Georges Wildenstein was tipped off, snatched it up for a pittance and managed to get it out of the country. A Louvre man was fired, and there was some flak in the French customs service, but Wildenstein was not troubled. He is said to have cleared about $700,000 on the sale; de La Tours are exceedingly rare. Some authorities, including Benedict Nicolson of *The Burlington Magazine*, have suggested that it might be a forgery, which would be ironic. Prevailing opinion, however, is that it's genuine. But I digress.)

"During that period," Ms Pearson went on, "a list for de-accessioning came down and the Ingres *Odalisque* was on it. I said, 'Gee, why?' Usually, they only de-accessioned

---

* John Buchanan, the registrar, vigorously denied that controls had weakened in any way, either before or after the layoffs. He said he knew all the time where the Ingres *Odalisque* was, for example, but would have referred any questions about it to museum headquarters upstairs. "This is not a policy office," he explained. Soon after our talk he was promoted to acting administrative assistant to Hoving to work on the "white paper."

stuff from the storerooms that nobody had ever seen. But that happens to be one of my favorite things in the museum. Well, somehow, it was taken off that list — apparently, a curator had flipped. But hang on. I found out later that the painting had been taken to Wildenstein. I asked why it hadn't been sent back, since I had no paper authorizing its de-accessioning. I was told to forget about it — it's a sensitive issue — and as far as I knew, when I left in June, the Ingres was still at Wildenstein."

The trail of the Ingres was an unexpected detour from my mission, which was to uncover, if possible, the truth about the Met's disposals of paintings already disclosed by Canaday. I had earlier studied the dossier, talked to a couple of museum people and listened to Hoving's defense. This was at a forum held at New York University in late November to consider the implications of the Met's secret dealings in art. Before a largely hostile if well-behaved audience, Hoving had been aloof and often disdainful, an attitude he would reveal by raising an eloquent eyebrow. He had, he said, participated over the years in the buying and selling of more than $280 million worth of art; the museum "knew exactly" what those French pictures would bring if they had been sold on the open market and exactly what their private sale "would bring us in future donations"; such sales are "a cool, dispassionate operation." The last phrase drew a murmur of protest, but he continued: "You have to go to somebody who has proven eyes . . . Some dealers have wonderful eyes . . . We do consult in every case with outside experts . . . I think our people goddam well know [what they're doing]."

Hoving was asked from the floor about the *Times*'s story that he had traded a Modigliani and a Juan Gris for a David Smith and (reportedly) a Clyfford Still. "We don't happen to own a Clyfford Still," he replied, adding that he would never have time to answer all the errors in the *Times*. Asked whether or not the public had a right to know what the terms were, he replied: "The public may be interested . . . but the Charter of the Metropolitan Museum states that every work of art is entirely owned by the trustees. There is no restriction whatever on the museum."

Since the pictures were "owned by the trustees," it seemed indicated that they be asked about them. I tried. President Dillon refused, from the beginning to the end of my inquiries, to answer any questions. Half a dozen elder trustees said they felt they could not honorably talk about what went on at board meetings, and hinted that it would be better for the museum if the *Times* did not pursue its investigations.

I abandoned efforts to penetrate the Club and turned to the people's representatives. Mayor Lindsay's office said he would reserve any comment for the board of trustees. Silence also from Controller Abe Beame and Parks Commissioner Richard M. Clurman, who with the mayor were ex officio trustees of the Met, and from Governor Rockefeller, an honorary trustee. Now, in enlarging the board membership to thirty-six, Hoving had added two representatives of the public, one a Harlem couturier, the other a Staten Island teacher. The former told me he could not comment "right off the top of my head," but would call me right back. He never did. The latter replied: "It's really not my area. Other areas I leave to the expertise of men like Mr. Dillon and Mr. Hoving, who I admire enormously."

Several former curators who had resigned from the Met declined to talk on the ground that their careers might be affected. A Park Avenue lady acknowledged that she had left a responsible post because she was unhappy about what was happening in her department, but refused to be quoted because "the last thing I want is to become a pariah." Dealers and artists told me they had to be discreet because they might have business with the Met. Nonetheless, bit by bit, I gathered information about the missing paintings — and more. But hardly anybody would talk for the record until Edith Pearson told me about the *Odalisque*.

I telephoned Louis Goldenberg, president of Wildenstein at its New York gallery and asked what he knew of the Ingres.

"I have no information as to what has happened," he replied.

Was it at Wildenstein's?

"Not to my knowledge."

Did he know whether it was for sale?

"The picture has never been offered us. [Pause.] There were other pictures offered us at one time."

I telephoned Curator Fahy and asked where the Odalisque was.

"I honestly don't know. You'll have to ask Mr. Hoving."

I did.

"It's in a place where it's being studied by specialists, about its true authorship," Hoving replied. "There is a broad group of specialists who hold that it's not by the master, and a few who believe it is. It is right in the middle of intense study."

Where?

"It is not in the museum."

Where is it, then?

"It's none of your business."

Pause. I suggested mildly that the public did have a right to know, and the *Times* was only trying to report the news.

"Frankly, I don't believe what you say. I think your balance is a little off."

Hoving then turned to the shortcomings of the *Times*'s cultural news department and especially of his "friend" the critic John Canaday. The director said he had already been informed that I was investigating him. Further, he added, he knew what my point of view was. Whenever possible, I turned the conversation back to the Ingres. "In the catalogue," Hoving said, "a number of scholars have questioned it . . . The painting's been away for a couple of months. It's not been on display for a long time . . . As soon as we get the information, we'll announce it . . ."

And finally —

"We believe that the picture is not by the master."

The story appeared in the *Times* cultural pages under a four-column headline:

METROPOLITAN FINDS 'ODALISQUE' NOT BY INGRES
WILL REHANG PAINTING WITH A NEW ATTRIBUTION

The same day, a curator called me — from a pay booth — and cried happily, "You've saved the Ingres!" With due credit to Edith Pearson, it is true that this story restored the *Odalisque* to the Met — but at the cost of her good name.

I of course checked the museum's published catalogue of French paintings. There was a photograph of the callipygous nude, familiar to museum-goers around the world, and a long article about it, but no reference to questions about its authenticity. On the contrary, it insisted that "there can be no doubt" that this was the *Odalisque in Gray* listed in Ingres's inventory as a preparatory work for the Louvre version, which is in color. The book suggested that the Met's painting might even be superior. The picture had, in fact, been in Ingres's studio at the time of his death, and its whereabouts accounted for at all times since. Some scholars had indeed wondered whether, as with so many old masters, Ingres had not sketched the painting out, allowed his assistants to fill it in, then gone over it at the end. But they deplored the fact that the painting had not been cleaned by the Met, which would have permitted proper analysis of the brushwork.

Hoving was a bit testy about the published story when I got back to him. "I said several times that it was being *studied* as to its condition and its authorship . . . We do have the name of the artist. It was Camon, C-a-m-o-n. We believe we have found an inventory . . . It's of poor quality. If you hang it alongside the original, you'll laugh. [He laughs.] It enables us to assemble the great body of works of Camon."

Theodore Rousseau, the Met's vice director and curator in chief, confided that it was he who had first noticed that there was something wrong about the *Odalisque*. It was right there, he said, visible even in a photograph — a "C" in a circle, under the lady's heel, and that was the monogram of Armand Cambon, Ingres's chief assistant.

"It makes me furious," he confessed, that he had never noticed it before. No, the picture had not been cleaned, because it was "in perfectly happy condition." Yes, "certainly" it had been de-accessioned, and it had been sent to Wildenstein, but not for sale, only for *expertise*. No, he could not recall another instance when the Met had sent a painting to a dealer for study, but Daniel Wildenstein of the Paris gallery was the greatest living authority on Ingres, having helped his father, Georges, write the definitive book. The *Odalisque* had gone to Paris but was now back, in customs.

Louis Goldenberg of Wildenstein in New York said no, and then, upon being told that Rousseau had said it was there, allowed that it was probably in a crate that had just arrived. He could not let us photograph it in its crate without the museum's permission. The Met said no, the insurance company would not allow it for security reasons. It might be helpful to crooks if they knew what the crate looked like.

John Connolly, a young art historian at Reed College in Oregon, snorted with derision. He said the well-known "C" mark under the *Odalisque*'s heel "discovered" by Rousseau was in fact a notation representing a waterspout that appears in the *Grande Odalisque* at the Louvre. In his opinion, this helped confirm the view that the Met painting was a preparatory study for the Louvre one. Connolly was irritated as well because when he visited the Met in early 1972 for another look at the picture, in connection with a study he has since published, he was told curtly that it was not available.

Back to Louis Goldenberg. He was unhappy about the Met's saying the *Odalisque* had been at Wildenstein, after all, and unhappier about its saying that it wasn't an Ingres. "We think their decision is wrong," he said. "We were quite surprised by it. I heard this morning that they found something by X ray. Our feeling was that the history was so solid . . . It has a marvelous pedigree."

Goldenberg said the gallery had never had a business interest in the *Odalisque* but was only studying it as a service to the museum, at no charge except for shipping and insurance. He estimated its value at up to $1 million.

In Paris, Andréas Freund of the *Times* called the Louvre. No, it had not seen the *Odalisque in Gray* nor been asked for its opinion. Freund called on Daniel Wildenstein. The dealer said his New York colleague was right; there was "no doubt whatsoever" that the painting was by Ingres. He said it could be proved easily if it were cleaned, but

Hoving had refused to let him do it. He differed with Goldenberg, however, on the valuation. Daniel thought the Ingres was worth about $300,000.

So the "world's leading authority on Ingres," who had been examining the *Odalisque* for a year in behalf of the Met, had found that she was as pure as the driven snow. Then on whose say-so was she now being called a chippie? Hoving and Rousseau would say no more. Nor would poor Curator Fahy, a specialist in Italian Renaissance paintings, who after my first story had told *Newsweek* that the *Odalisque* was probably not by Ingres, and after my second told his friends that he had been mistaken after all.

Weeks later I learned from one of those unimpeachable but also unquotable sources in the museum that the *Odalisque* had, of course, been given to Wildenstein in a commercial deal as part payment against another painting. Wildenstein had long enjoyed mutually profitable dealings with the museum, but it could hardly disavow an Ingres painting that it had been trying to sell. As it happened, the deal had not been fully closed, and when the *Times* began asking embarrassing questions, the *Odalisque* was hastily recalled. I could not find out anything more, but no matter. The lady was back at the Met and, though her complexion had not yet been cleaned of its grime, her reputation was spotless.

Which could not be said of the Met.

POSTSCRIPT: After this chapter was written the museum confirmed, in its "white paper" of June 20, 1973, that the *Odalisque* had indeed been offered to Wildenstein in exchange for a part interest in another painting. It did not disclose the valuation, nor explain why the deal had been denied. It said the sale of the *Odalisque* fell through "because the Museum insisted that doubts about its authen-

ticity be stated by Wildenstein in any future transaction."
(As will be seen, the Met had no such scruples regarding
other "suspect" paintings it had sold.) The white paper
also said that Rousseau and Fahy were "more certain than
ever that the Museum's *Odalisque* is a workshop copy of
the *Grande Odalisque* in the Louvre although there re-
mains a possibility that Ingres may have done certain parts
of it . . . However, since it is an attractive work of some
art historical interest which has been improved by cleaning,
it has been reaccessioned." The *Odalisque* again hangs in
the Met, over the legend "Ingres and Workshop."

CHAPTER 10

Buy Dear, Sell Cheap

It has been further alleged that the Metropolitan sold Rousseau's *Tropics* and Van Gogh's *Olive Pickers* for too little. The Acquisitions Committee on the Board of Trustees took every step necessary to attain the best price possible at the time, an amount which exceeded the prior estimate of one of the leading auction galleries. Secondly, the two paintings by Gris and Modigliani also mentioned in the press were evaluated by two prominent New York art dealers prior to their being exchanged for other fine works of equivalent value by important artists not represented in our collection.

— Thomas Hoving, in a letter to the *Times*,
October 31, 1972

The cover-up by the Met administration was crumbling. Informants came forward with proof that Canaday had told the truth — for example, records showing that the Met had de-accessioned the great Picasso, Cézanne, Gauguin, two Monets and many others, and re-accessioned them only after Canaday had reported they were being sold.

It was, of course, no surprise. Nor was it surprising to learn that the Met had *not* sought expert opinion in the sale of the van Gogh and the Rousseau, nor in the sale of some other paintings Canaday was not aware of, and that the prices obtained were contestable indeed.

What *was* surprising was a tip about the swap of art with

Marlborough. An informant said the Met had given the gallery not only the Modigliani *Red Head* and the Juan Gris *Guéridon,* but also another Gris, *Harlequin,* a Bonnard nude, a 1923 Picasso still-life and a Renoir oil sketch of roses.

Not two, but six modern French masters in an even exchange for two contemporary Americans works. These were a ten-foot-high abstract sculpture, essentially six rectangles of stainless steel welded together, by the late David Smith, and a large beige canvas painted by Richard Diebenkorn. (It was not until later that I learned that the original deal called for a Clyfford Still, but Frank Lloyd of Marlborough had asked an even higher price, so the Diebenkorn was thrown in instead as a make weight. Canaday was not wrong about the Still, after all.)

The source was reliable, but the tip was hard to believe. Donald McKinney, vice president of Marlborough, told me I was mistaken: "The transaction did not include a Clyfford Still *nor* a Diebenkorn"; but added, "I don't have the facts — Mr. Lloyd made the arrangement." He said he hadn't even seen the French paintings, because they had been shipped to Europe the day after they arrived at Marlborough.

In the registrar's office at the Met, a female employee showed me the card files; all six de Groot paintings were still listed as part of the museum collections. Since Hoving had conceded that the Modigliani and the Juan Gris had been disposed of, I found this mystifying.

I telephoned Ashton Hawkins, the blond young secretary of the museum.

"I don't have the information, but wouldn't tell if I did," he replied.

I said I was just trying to set the record straight on the deal reported by Canaday.

HAWKINS (airily): He made it up.

HESS (quietly, very Coldstream Guards): I suggest you withdraw that remark.

HAWKINS: Huh?

HESS (grimly): I suggest you withdraw that remark.

HAWKINS: Well, his facts were wrong.

In retrospect, the dialogue seems fairly absurd, but at the time I was really angry. Hawkins finally promised to check about the de Groot paintings and call back, but he did not. So the next day, I called upon a Very Important Person in the financial-political-cultural Establishment — a man of such status that he required me not to reveal that he had received me. I put it to him that the practice of concealing the Met's transactions and of insulting journalists who disclosed them could only damage the museum. He agreed. After making a telephone call, he advised me that the Met was now ready to put the facts on the table.

My appointment was with Theodore Rousseau, the chief curator, but Hoving himself met me in shirtsleeves, putting a friendly arm on my shoulder. "You really upset our security service," he said with a smile. "And I guess you found that our records were not quite up to date." (It developed that although I had identified myself, I was not supposed to have had access to the index files that had been shown me. They were subsequently locked away, from scholars as well as reporters.)

Hoving acknowledged that the policy of secrecy might have outlived its time and said the trustees would consider modifying it. Meanwhile, though, he would tell me what pictures had been disposed of — but not their price.

"We never talk about what we pay for things, and we never talk about what we get for things," he said.

Nor would Hoving reveal what paintings had been de-accessioned or re-accessioned. But he did confirm that the

Met had given the six de Groot paintings for the David Smith *Becca* and the Diebenkorn *Ocean Park #30*.

Hoving emphasized that the French paintings were little ones, and inferior to boot, whereas the David Smith was "dazzling" and "one of our most welcome pieces."

"The *Becca* was offered twice to the board of trustees, who liked it enormously, but we simply didn't have the money," he said.

Rousseau recalled that the sculpture first was offered at $100,000. This was before it was installed in the Met's centennial show, *New York Painting and Sculpture: 1940–1970*. Hoving said this helped to increase its value, and subsequent offerings were at $150,000, then $200,000. I filed it away that the Met had increased the cost of a purchase simply by having shown it on loan, and asked if anything else of Miss de Groot's had been sold.

Rousseau said that early in 1972 the Met had disposed of thirty-two minor things, in a private auction with sealed bids. (This is a device associated with the Museum of Modern Art; when MOMA wants to sell pictures quietly, it invites a number of dealers to a rendezvous, shows them the pictures and collects their bids in envelopes. Just one bid to a painting, and the top bid wins.)

Departing, I asked whether there were any other unreported sales of valuable paintings. Hoving asked Rousseau, and the curator shook his head. Hoving said no.

My article on the disposal of more de Groot paintings put the Met back under a spotlight, all the harsher because I quoted Miss de Groot's will, asking that her paintings not be sold. But in a radio interview and in a telephone call to me, Hoving said my story, unlike preceding ones in the *Times*, had been "balanced and excellent." However, perhaps to his surprise, I did not feel that the picture was complete.

Checking around, I found that the Met had modified the MOMA procedure on private auctions. Rather than have the dealers in all at once, it had invited five or six in turn to look at the thirty-two pictures.

A dealer I shall call Joe recounts that he telephoned Henry Geldzahler, the curator of twentieth-century paintings, and said he had learned that some pictures were for sale and would like to look at them; "I'm sorry, Joe," Henry said gently, "you're not on the list."

Those who were on the list put in bids for the pictures they liked. A lot of them were very minor ones, they recall, and most of the bids concentrated on the best names: a Léger, two De Chiricos, a Dufy and so on; the best single bid I heard of was $20,000. The bids were opened in Ashton Hawkins' office, so nobody else knew what the others had offered. The lot was awarded to Harold Diamond, a private dealer.*

Diamond told me he had paid "well below $100,000" for the collection, and that "it was no big deal." When the paintings were delivered to him, he said, "I turned positively green."

"It's a miracle," he said, "I sold most of them."

One of those he sold was a John Kane landscape that the Carnegie Institute had long wanted, because the school appears in it. It got a good price, as undoubtedly did a number of other "name" pictures.

"I'm not rich from it," Diamond said. "But it was fun — a test of my ability. The Metropolitan did very well on my deal. If anybody should complain, it's me. They never even offered any of the other stuff to me. But what the hell — you gotta take the good with the bad."

* Months later, it transpired that Diamond had first bid $48,825 for five paintings, and had then been persuaded in private negotiations to make a new bid and take all thirty-two for $80,000. Some auction . . . Geldzahler had appraised the lot at $94,600.

The "other stuff" was indeed more interesting. Dealers who had seen most of the six pictures given to Marlborough guessed their market value at $400,000. But the pictures were gone and neither the Met nor Marlborough would reveal their price.

One could get at it, however, another way.

Diebenkorn, it was learned, had been paid $13,500 for his painting, less a commission of 40 per cent. Actually, the list price was $15,000, a very good price for a Diebenkorn, but the Met was granted a museum discount of 10 per cent. (Dealers' discounts to museums often run to 20 per cent. As for living artists, they are often happy to donate works outright, for promotional reasons. Geldzahler's gallery at the Met hangs several such gifts.)

Essentially, David Smith's *Becca* was what the swap was about. Since the late sculptor's daughters were still minors, the estate was in the hands of three executors: Ira Lowe, a lawyer; Robert Motherwell, the artist, and Clement Greenberg, the critic.

As a lawyer, Lowe granted readily that the affairs of the estate were a matter of public record. He said Marlborough had reported to the estate that it had sold the *Becca* for $225,000. After taking its commission of 25 per cent, the gallery had paid Lowe the net, $168,750.

This was remarkable on several counts. It was by far the highest price ever paid for a David Smith. The previous record was thought in the trade to be $80,000, paid by the Des Moines Art Center, but Lowe revealed that Pepsico had paid Marlborough $150,000 for another Smith.[*]

Motherwell, too, thought the sale to the Met was a "marvelous deal." But both he and Lowe were surprised to

---

[*] Emily Genauer, the art critic, later described the $225,000 price as "astonishingly generous" and quoted Joseph Hirshhorn, who has probably bought more American sculpture than any other man, as having said that any price over $150,000 was absurd.

hear that Marlborough had swapped the sculpture for French paintings. They said they had been told it was a cash deal.

Both said Greenberg handled the business end of the estate. The critic told me: "The asking price had been $250,000 — and it was set by the estate — and the estate came down to $225,000. I don't know what else Marlborough does. I want to give Marlborough a clean bill on this; they behaved very well."

Unlike the other executors, Greenberg said he had been aware that some kind of swap had occurred. "I assume that they received still more than covered the cost of the Smith," the critic said. "That's none of my business. The estate got the money it was asking for."

As a lawyer, Lowe saw the problem differently. Marlborough had a contract as exclusive selling agent for the Smith estate at a commission of 25 per cent. Now if Marlborough got *more* than the sum it had reported to the estate — even though that sum was precisely what the estate had asked — then the executors were obliged to collect the difference. A living artist may waive his rights; an executor is more limited. Lowe said he would look into the matter. "I certainly want to be correct," Lowe said. "If they received more than what I know, then that is part of the estate, as far as I am concerned. I intend to do whatever is necessary."

(The director of a major institution, stunned by the price cited, said: "A museum doesn't *buy* a David Smith, it is *given* one." A collector demanded: "If they wanted a Smith, why didn't they swap for it with the Albright in Buffalo?" A prominent dealer commented: "There are dozens of David Smiths around, but try and get a good Modigliani!")

At any rate, we now were able to report the nominal

value of the swap: $225,000 for the David Smith plus $13,500 for the Diebenkorn equaled $238,500. For this the Met had given Marlborough a Modigliani, two Grises, a Bonnard, a Picasso and a Renoir, thought in the trade to be worth up to $400,000.

Reached just in time to make the edition of the *Times* reporting this, Chief Curator Rousseau termed the dealers' estimates "exaggerated" and "a matter of opinion."

"We've got a record of outside appraisals," he said.

The new Met policy of candor still had a few days to go. Rousseau promised to release the appraisals with a list of art sold by the museum over the last two years, and he was as good as his word.

The dark, handsome and usually debonair Rousseau, who usually looked far younger than his sixty years, was wan and tired when I called on him. With Hoving abroad on one of several holidays he took during the crisis, the chief curator was in charge of the museum.

"What really sparked all this," he told me, "was the acquisition of a really great work of art — the Velázquez. We had to make some sacrifices."

Couldn't they raise the $5,544,000 by donations?

"We tried, but it wasn't easy."

He repeated that, contrary to what Marlborough had been suggesting, the deal for the David Smith had been a straight swap. A sale to the Met for cash and a simultaneous purchase of paintings from the Met for cash would have put the gallery in the clear as to the price paid the Smith estate. But no money had changed hands.

"I like that kind of transaction," Rousseau said. "It made it possible for the dealer to fudge his coming down in price."

"All of a sudden," he added ruefully, "you've got this Japanese buying. Consequently [prices having risen sharply] we look as though we made a bad deal."

He handed me three photocopies. One was an undated, unsigned typewritten sheet, purported to list the valuations of the six French pictures by Henry Geldzahler, the curator of twentieth-century art. They came to $240,000, only $1,500 higher than Marlborough's price for the Smith and the Diebenkorn.

The second, also undated, was signed by dealer Harold Diamond, the man who had bought the thirty-two minor de Groot pictures. He valued five of the six pictures at $193,000, and an unknown hand had penciled in $16,000 more for the Renoir (Fahy had estimated it at $20,000).

(Diamond said he had understood he was making a bid on the five paintings, and thought this was long before the other appraisals . . . The Renoir was an afterthought in the deal. Another dealer later showed me a letter he had written the museum long before, in which he estimated he could sell that painting for it at $25,000.)

The third sheet was a memorandum by Rousseau, dated June 8, 1972 — four days before the trustees approved the swap with Marlborough. Whether or not they were aware of this memo could not be learned. It read:

> This afternoon Roland Balaÿ of Knoedler Galleries came to look at the paintings recommended for de-accessioning by the Department of Twentieth Century Art and appraised them as follows:

BONNARD	Nude	$ 55/60,000
GRIS	Le Guéridon	40,000
GRIS	Harlequin	40,000
MODIGLIANI	Red Head	150,000
PICASSO	Still Life	45,000

To the list $16,000 more had been anonymously added for the Renoir.

Conclusion: the president of one of the world's leading

art galleries had appraised the paintings at $346,000 to $351,000 only a few days before the Met gave them to Marlborough for a nominal price of $238,500.

Rousseau anticipated my question.

He noted that the difference between Knoedler's total and the others was accounted for largely by the Modigliani. Balaÿ figured it was worth $150,000, while Geldzahler figured it at $50,000. (Diamond had offered $65,000, but was ignored.)

"Knoedler was not aware that there is a near version of the Modigliani," he said.

He showed me a catalogue of an auction at Sotheby, held in that same month of June 1972. There was a portrait of that same redhead. (It sold, I later learned, for $293,250, which was well above what the Met got for its Modigliani and five other paintings.)

Where there is such duplication, Rousseau said, "You're afraid of a fake."

Fake. The word had only been whispered, in defense of the sale of the Douanier Rousseau *Tropics,* and implied with respect to the authorship of the missing Ingres *Odalisque.* Now it was openly tagged to a painting that the Met had sold for $50,000.

Half a dozen experts hooted that Modigliani had often painted several versions of the same subject. Klaus Perls, the dealer who had featured the Modigliani in his 1958 show of de Groot paintings — for which Rousseau had written the glowing introduction — was ready to stake a fortune on its authenticity. And by telephone from Paris Roland Balaÿ told me indignantly: "My opinion and my appraisal remain exactly the same today." Balaÿ said he had been "perfectly aware that a near version of the Modigliani" was being sold at Sotheby.

"The Modigliani I saw at the Metropolitan Museum is

genuine and is worth about $150,000,"* he added. "Furthermore, I am sure that if the Metropolitan Museum had been afraid of a fake, they would not have sold it to the Marlborough Gallery.

"Having been a dealer in modern painting for 50 years and president of Knoedler for 18, it seems to me that my judgment should not be lightly disregarded."

Curator Geldzahler disagreed.

"I've always been frankly embarrassed by that picture," he told me. "It's no good. I would say it's on the cusp between really, really bad Modigliani and no Modigliani at all."

What would a Modigliani on the cusp be worth?

"I don't know. I must have said fifty or sixty thousand . . ."

Did Marlborough know of this doubt about the picture?

"Yes, I gave Frank Lloyd a letter stating that should it turn out that the Modigliani was indeed a fake, he would be reimbursed to the extent of $60,000 cash."

So Lloyd couldn't lose, and the Met couldn't win. If the Modigliani were genuine, he had a $150,000 picture for $50,000 — which was Geldzahler's original valuation. If it were fake, the Met would buy it back for $60,000. (The $10,000 discrepancy was never explained.)

To another question, Geldzahler replied: "I would think that Frank could get eighty-five or ninety thousand for this picture, which is a normal dealer's markup."

The remark supported the observation of a number of critics: when the museum sells to dealers, it gets wholesale prices, while when it buys from dealers, it pays retail prices.

Buy dear, sell cheap.

* *Time* later reported that Marlborough had sold the Modigliani in Japan for $200,000.

CHAPTER II

Henry, Clem and Andy

The Museum of Modern Art has the most extraordinary
collection of European modern masters in the world. I'd
prefer to collect in areas where the MOMA is less strong.

— Henry Geldzahler, curator of twentieth-century art
at the Metropolitan, in an interview with the author

When young Tom Hoving, the swinging parks commissioner of New York, was named director of the Met,
young Henry Geldzahler let his beard grow back. The
late director James J. Rorimer had made Henry shave it off
when he joined the Met in 1960. As it was, the older man
felt pretty venturesome when he hired a twenty-five-year-
old guru of the Harvard coffee houses; according to Calvin
Tomkins, he also advised Henry not to let on to the
trustees that he was Jewish. Henry had turned down his
offer at first, explaining that he was interested in contemporary American art — which the Met was not — and really
wanted to work for the Whitney, one of three New York
museums devoted to that field. But that job was not
available, so Henry shaved his beard.

His life style did not change, however. Within months
of his arrival, the cherubic Henry had become a panjan-
drum of the New York Pop Art scene, visiting all the studios
by day, making all the "in" parties by night, interviewed
by all the with-it journals. (Asked by Frances FitzGerald
for the secret to his success, he said, "I like Marshall
McLuhan's definition: a celebrity is wellknown from being

wellknown.") When Hoving staged his happenings in the parks, he was years behind Henry, who had *starred* in the first happenings. Now the two of them would bring the staid old Met into the Swinging Sixties.

This improbable marriage of the old social establishment with the parvenu art crowd came to climax in October 1969 at the *vernissage* of Henry's show *New York Paintings and Sculpture: 1940–1970*. A fine account was given by Calvin Tomkins in an affectionate Profile of Henry that he wrote for *The New Yorker* while working on the history of the museum commissioned by the Met. Geldzahler lent me a copy of the Profile, calling it the best of all those written about him. Tomkins described that night of October 18, 1969, as follows:

> The stately, black-tie world of the Metropolitan trustees found itself mingling with tribal swingers dressed as American Indians, frontiersmen, Cossacks, Restoration rakes, gypsies, houris, and creatures of purest fantasy. The see-through blouse achieved its apotheosis that night, and spectators lined up three-deep to observe the action on the dance floor — there was a rock band in one gallery and a dance orchestra in another, to say nothing of six strategically placed bars. Works of sculpture acquired festoons of empty plastic glasses, the reek of marijuana hung heavy in the air, and at one point in the evening, while the rock group blasted away in a room full of Frank Stella's paintings and David Smith's sculptures, a tall woman and a lame sculptor wrestled for fifteen minutes on the parquet floor, untroubled by guards, spectators or a century of Metropolitan decorum. Exhilaration was everywhere, compounded of pride, chauvinism, and sheer visual delight. The New York School had wrested the mantle of artistic supremacy from Paris (as one was forever being reminded).

Not everyone was exhilarated. The art critics, in fact, were virtually unanimous in decrying Henry's show. Canaday of the *Times* called it "a booboo on a grand scale" and "an inadequately masked declaration of the Museum's sponsorship of an esthetic-political-commercial power combine promoted by the Museum's Achilles' heel, Henry Geldzahler." Katherine Kuh in the *Saturday Review* said the huge "hot-off-the-griddle" pictures chosen by Henry "often seem little more than superbly designed backdrops for a glittering world of 'beautiful people' who somehow forgot to appear." Harold Rosenberg of *The New Yorker* said the exhibition was "tone-deaf" and, "in its indifference to the personages, from de Kooning to Nakian and Steinberg, who have reduced the gap that separates New York from Paris of the past, 'Henry's Show' makes art in America seem in a more precarious position than it is."

All the critics remarked on the omissions from a monumental show with such an ambitious title as *New York Paintings and Sculpture: 1940–1970*. There were forty-two Ellsworth Kellys and twenty-two David Smiths, but almost nothing from the first two decades of that period, and nothing at all from some of the biggest figures of New York, 1940 to 1970. They noted also that Henry had snubbed Pop Art, which he had so helped to "discover."

Hoving backed Henry's judgments in a statement that typically, as Rosenberg observed, "turned itself inside out before the reader's eyes." In a foreword to the show's catalogue, Hoving wrote: "Although it is conceivable that no two people would have picked anywhere near the same works of art . . . it is highly unlikely."

Geldzahler explained his philosophy in the catalogue's introduction, written like all his formal utterances in a drily pedantic style that surprises all who know his informal discourse. "As curator," he wrote, "my guiding principles in deciding which artists to include in the exhibition . . . have been the extent to which their work has commanded critical attention or significantly deflected the course of recent art."

"We must presume then," retorted Miss Kuh, "that his choices were directed less by his own convictions than by those of the critics he admires. Or possibly it is these critics, especially Clement Greenberg, who seem to have formed his convictions. So why not have Mr. Greenberg do the show?"

In a sense, perhaps Greenberg did. Tomkins quoted Geldzahler as saying: "I feel that he's the best critic we've ever had, and that if I disagree with him I'm probably wrong."

The statement takes on added significance if one is aware that Greenberg is on a "visiting committee" of experts who advise Geldzahler on the buying, selling and hanging of art at the Met.

Greenberg is one of the two figures most closely associated with Geldzahler as arbiters of the sixties art scene in New York. The other was Andy Warhol. "Was" is correct, because while Henry was one of the first to discover Andy and his Pop-and-Gay scene, he was also, along with Greenberg, one of the first to drop him.

"For six years," Geldzahler told Tomkins, "every day would begin with a telephone conversation with Andy and end the same way." In between, Henry spent a lot of time in Andy's studio; Warhol's first movie was a short showing Henry brushing his teeth, which led to a full-length feature of Henry smoking a cigar. But they broke up in 1966, when Henry left Andy out of his selections for the Venice Biennale and wrote on a blackboard in the studio, "Andy can't paint anymore, and he can't make movies yet." Of these incidents, Tomkins wrote: "Some people accused him of becoming a mere acolyte of Greenberg's circle — which was known informally as the Kosher Nostra. It was sometimes said that Henry's eyes weren't too good but his ears were great. The truth was that Henry, as usual, was just being himself. Only recently had it begun to occur to people that Henry's true self was essentially conservative."

In another context, Geldzahler put it differently. "I'm always asked," he said, "what's going to happen next in art, and I usually paraphrase what Bob Rauschenberg once said: 'I don't know, but I hope I'm in it.' What I say is, 'I don't know, but I hope I'll recognize it.'"

As he often did, he was echoing Greenberg, who in *his* article in the Geldzahler catalogue refers to "something new, therefore worth saying." Representational art was in, then out, then in again. Abstract expressionism was in, then out; pop was in, then out. As Henry put it, "It seems today that Pop art was an episode." That meant that Warhol was out.

Which may explain why the night of Henry's *vernissage*, Andy loitered on the steps of the Met and, when asked why he didn't go in, replied: "I'm the *first* Mrs. Geldzahler."

Henry was not the only swinger at the Met, only the most engagingly candid. Still, times have changed. The March 1973 issue of *Andy Warhol's Interview* features a sprightly chat with John McKendry, the Met's curator of prints, his wife, Maxime de la Falaise, and her daughter, Lulu. They rated cover treatment as among the "best-dressed" of the jet set, and McKendry was described as "internationally renowned for his taste for luxuries of every sort." The dialogue is bush-league Oscar Wilde: McKendry suggests that he, Maxime and Lulu be asked about incest, and says, "Yeah, I'm incestuous" — an in joke for those who know them. His father, he said, had reproached him for being "a plaything of the rich." McKendry added: "My father believes in Labor and the Catholic Church. I believe in neither. I believe in the very rich."

Money, fun and status were the themes of the art scene of the sixties — such status as the taxi tycoon Robert Scull could obtain when Hoving hung at the Met his huge billboard by James Rosenquist, *F–111*. A small group of artists and dealers profited vastly. Most of them had one thing in common: the approval of Clement Greenberg.

The scene has been well described by Sophy Burnham in the book *The Art Crowd*. Many art critics and curators didn't like it; they complained that she just didn't understand why artists gave valuable works to people who wrote nice things about them and hung their pictures in museums. Mrs. Burnham's implication that this might be naughty was roundly trounced by one Sam Hunter of Princeton in the *New York Times Book Review*. The passage is worth reprinting in its entirety

> Another example of misguided muckraking is the insistence that critics refuse gifts of works of art from artists whom they are presenting in print, presumably in a major article or monograph. The admonition ignores not only a long-standing tradition of reciprocal appreciation dating back at least to the Impressionists, but more important, it mechanizes and degrades the relationship between serious artists and their critics. The allegiance is of necessity partisan, and the product of mutual intellectual infatuation; yet it is entirely idealistic and pure in motive. No responsible critic would violate his own sensibilities, or alter a syllable of prose on the basis of some proffered or withheld art gift.

One hesitates to gloss this superb passage; it is Biblical in its condensation of an ethic and a culture. The work of art is equated with the critique for which it is given — "presumably a major article or monograph"! — and only a Philistine would consider the former to be superior. Indeed, in the age when Nothing may be Art, the critique may well be worth more.

Bury St. Edmunds Cross, XII century. The Metropolitan Museum of Art, the Cloisters Collection, 1963.

"He first topped the British bid, then sat with the Yugoslav in a café until the British option expired at midnight. Five minutes later the Cross belonged to the Metropolitan Museum of Art."

Velázquez, *Philip IV, King of Spain*, XVII century. The Metropolitan Museum of Art, Bequest of Benjamin Altman, 1913.

"The most prominent of the demoted canvases was the portrait of Philip IV" which the curator declared could not be a Velázquez. Subsequently, experts refuted his evidence and the Velázquez was rehabilitated.

Rembrandt Harmensz van Ryn, *Aristotle Contemplating the Bust of Homer*, 1653. The Metropolitan Museum of Art. Purchased with special funds and gifts of friends of the Museum, 1961.

"The purchase of the Rembrandt *Aristotle* was debated in the board for weeks before the auction. Retroactive approval [for an acquisition] was an innovation of the Hoving regime."

Pablo Picasso, *Woman in White*, 1923. The Metropolitan Museum of Art, Rogers Fund, 1951; from the Museum of Modern Art, Lillie P. Bliss Collection.

". . . records showed that the Met had 'de-accessioned' Picasso, Cézanne, Gauguin, Monet, and many others, and 're-accessioned' them only after Canaday (in the *Times*) had reported they were being sold."

Jean Auguste Dominique Ingres, *Odalisque in Grisaille*, XIX century.
The Metropolitan Museum of Art, Wolfe Fund, 1938.

"We believe that the picture is not by the master but '. . . when the
Times began asking embarrassing questions, the *Odalisque* was hastily
recalled.' "

Velázquez, *Portrait of Juan de Pareja*, 1650. The Metropolitan Museum of Art, Isaac D. Fletcher Fund, Rogers Fund and Bequest of Adelaide Milton de Groot (1876–1967), Bequest of Joseph H. Durkee, by exchange, supplemented by gifts from friends of the Museum, 1971.

"Wildenstein got the portrait [for the Met] for the highest price ever paid at a picture auction: $5,544,000 . . . except for [Douglas] Dillon, *the trustees did not know that they had bought a Velázquez!*"

Edouard Manet, *A Boy with a Sword*. The Metropolitan Museum of Art, Gift of Erwin Davis, 1889.

"One might think that putting Henry [Geldzahler] in charge of the French masters was like getting a fox to guard the hen house . . . except that he looked more like a teddy bear."

Georges de La Tour, *The Fortune Teller (L'Enfant Prodigue ou La Bonne Aventure)*. The Metropolitan Museum of Art, Rogers Fund, 1960.

"The painting had been spotted by the Louvre in a chateau in the Anjou, but the late Georges Wildenstein was tipped off, snatched it up for a pittance and managed to get it out of the country . . . He is said to have cleared $700,000 on the sale."

Opposite Pablo Picasso, *The Coiffure*. The Metropolitan Museum of Art, Wolfe Fund, 1951. Acquired from the Museum of Modern Art, Anonymous Gift.

" 'We cleaned *The Coiffure* and it turned out to be a much better picture than we had suspected,' Geldzahler said."

Vincent van Gogh, *Potato Peeler*. The Metropolitan Museum of Art, Bequest of Adelaide Milton de Groot (1876–1967), 1967.

Many paintings in Adelaide de Groot's collection were minor ones, but a few were quite important, particularly the van Gogh self-portrait with the *Potato Peeler* on the reverse side.

Eugene Delacroix, *Le Panier de Fleurs (Cornucopia)*, 1848. From the collection of Adelaide Milton de Groot. (Courtesy of the Perls Galleries, N.Y.)

". . . Without limiting in any way the absolute nature of this bequest, I request said Metropolitan Museum of Art not to sell any of said works of art . . ." (Part of a clause in Adelaide de Groot's will leaving her paintings to the Metropolitan Museum of Art. At least fifty of her paintings have been sold.)

Edouard Manet, *Portrait de Madame Manet,* c. 1867. From the collection of Adelaide Milton de Groot. (Courtesy of the Perls Galleries, N.Y.)

"An artist who had married money once confided to me bitterly that it was a hard way to make a dollar. In that sense, the Metropolitan Museum may be said to have fairly earned the fortune it got from Adelaide Milton de Groot."

Henri de Toulouse-Lautrec, *L'Anglais au Moulin Rouge*, 1892.
From the collection of Adelaide Milton de Groot (Courtesy of
the Perls Galleries, N.Y.)

"When she wanted to revisit those of her pictures hanging at the
Met . . . she would telephone ahead and be met at the door by the
director or by the handsome young Ted Rousseau and an underling
or two, with a wheelchair in later years, and be taken on a guided
tour."

Thomas Eakins, *Arcadia*, c. 1885. From the collection of Adelaide Milton de Groot. (Courtesy of the Perls Galleries, N.Y.)

"She was touched when Rorimer appeared at her door one Thanksgiving day with a turkey dinner in a basket, and sat with her while she ate it."

Amedeo Modigliani, *La Rousse*, 1918. The Metropolitan Museum of
Art, Bequest of Miss Adelaide Milton de Groot (1876–1967), 1967.

After sale of many of the paintings, Mr. Rousseau said they were "a lot
of junk" and the Modigliani (*above*) was possibly a fake.

Fernand Léger, *Le Printemps*, 1929. From the collection of Adelaide Milton de Groot. (Courtesy of the Perls Galleries, N.Y.)

"In 1958, Rousseau helped mount a charity show of *Masterpieces from the Adelaide Milton de Groot Collection* at the Perls Galleries. He wrote a glowing preface to the catalogue, which appeared alongside a reproduction of Modigliani's *Red Head* — the very one he later denounced."

" 'If that Rousseau was so lousy, why did they send it to us in their *100 Masterpieces* show?' "

Henri Rousseau, *Tropiques*, c. 1907. From the collection of Adelaide Milton de Groot. (Courtesy of the Perls Galleries, N.Y.)

"Two daughters of the late Sam Lewisohn . . . told museum officials that they were shocked to learn that their father's Gauguin and Renoir were being put on the market. They said remaining masterpieces in their hands would never be left to the museum if that happened."

Paul Gauguin, *Nature Morte*, 1891. From the collection of Adelaide Milton de Groot. (Courtesy of the Perls Galleries, N.Y.)

Claude Monet, *Bordighera*, 1884. From the collection of Adelaide Milton de Groot. (Courtesy of the Perls Galleries, N.Y.)

" 'At one point . . . I had fourteen Monets on a list for de-accessioning. I don't know what the final decision was.' "

Maurice Utrillo, *Le Moulin à Montmartre*, 1912. From the collection of Adelaide Milton de Groot. (Courtesy of the Perls Galleries, N.Y.)

"If the Met must sell art, they said, it should do it in the open, explain its reasons and give first preference to other museums as buyers, and second preference to the open market, 'so that maximum proceeds are assured.'"

Chaim Soutine, *Portrait de Madame Marcel Castaing*, 1928. From the collection of Adelaide Milton de Groot. (Courtesy of the Perls Galleries, N.Y.)

"Several former curators who had resigned from the Met declined to talk on the ground that their careers might be affected. A Park Avenue lady acknowledged that she had left a responsible post because she was unhappy about what was happening in her department, but refused to be quoted because 'the last thing I want is to become a pariah.'"

Raoul Dufy, *Vue de Nice*, 1929. From the collection of Adelaide Milton de Groot. (Courtesy of the Perls Galleries, N.Y.)

"Having had to re-accession the lot of French masters they had originally chosen, the Hoving team set out to find replacements."

Amedeo Modigliani, *Portrait de Juan Gris*, 1916. From the collection of Adelaide Milton de Groot. (Courtesy of the Perls Galleries, N.Y.)

" 'Decisions on how, when and where to sell require great knowledge, experience, and intuition. Most knowledgeable persons agree that the museum is very well qualified to make such decisions and has been making them successfully for decades.' "

Opposite The Met traded van der Heyden's painting to Weitzner for one (*below*) by Saraceni, a lesser-known master of the Italian Renaissance. The Saraceni had cost Weitzner $1152. He later resold the van der Heyden, which was in terrible condition, for six figures.

Jan van der Heyden, *A Street in Delft,*

Carlo Saraceni, *Community of the Blessed Adoring the Holy Trinity.*

Henri Matisse, *Odalisque*, 1923. From the collection of Adelaide Milton de Groot. (Courtesy of the Perls Galleries, N.Y.)

" 'I don't give a damn what anybody says,' Lloyd observed. 'There's only one measure of success in running a gallery: making money. Any dealer who says it's not is a hypocrite or will soon be closing his doors.' "

Opposite Juan Gris, *L'Arlequin*, 1918. The Metropolitan Museum of Art, Bequest of Miss Adelaide Milton de Groot (1876–1967), 1967.

"We now were able to report the nominal value of the swap: $225,000 for the David Smith plus $13,500 for the Diebenkorn equaled $238,500. For this the Met had given Marlborough a Modigliani, two Gris, a Bonnard, a Picasso and a Renoir, thought in the trade to be worth up to $400,000."

David Smith, *Becca*, 1965. The Metropolitan Museum of Art, Bequest of Adelaide Milton de Groot (1876–1967), 1967.

A director, stunned by the $225,000 price tag, exclaimed that "a museum doesn't buy a David Smith, it is *given* one."

Pablo Picasso, *Tête de Femme*, c. 1903. From the collection of Adelaide Milton de Groot. (Courtesy of the Perls Galleries, N.Y.)

" 'Somebody would phone from the entry and say a "Mister So-and-So is here from a gallery" — Wildenstein or another — "with a painting, and asks for a receipt. We didn't know it was out of the building.' "

Georges Braque, *Nature Morte*, 1929. From the collection of Adelaide Milton de Groot. (Courtesy of the Perls Galleries, N.Y.)

"Canaday recalled that the Chicago Art Institute had sold a lot of Monets in 1944 for less than it would pay for one of them today, that the Minneapolis Institute of Arts had unloaded a treasure of old masters for a song, that the Guggenheim would be glad to have back the 97 Kandinskys it had sold."

Annibale Carracci, *Coronation of the Virgin*, c. 1596. The Metropolitan Museum of Art. Purchase, Bequest of Adelaide Milton de Groot
(1876–1967), and Dr. and Mrs. Manuel Porter and Sons, Gift in honor
of Mrs. Sarah Porter, 1971.

The proceeds gained from the sale of the French Impressionists went for
the upgrading of the collections, notably for a Velázquez and for Carracci's *Coronation of the Virgin*.

Vincent van Gogh, *The Olive Pickers*, 1889.

"It had once belonged to the late Vincent Astor, two of whose successive wives, Mrs. Brooke Astor and Mrs. Minnie Fosburgh, now sat on the Acquisitions Committee."

Euphronios, Black-figured calyx krater: *The Death of Sarpedon*, Greek vase VI century B.C. The Metropolitan Museum of Art, Bequest of Joseph H. Durkee, Gift of Darius Ogden Mills and Gift of C. Ruxton Love, by exchange.

" 'When I saw the vase,' he said, 'I knew I had found what I had been searching for all my life.' "

" 'Unless you're naive or not very bright, you'd have to know that much ancient art is stolen.' "

Euxitheos and Euphronios, Red-figured calyx krater: *Warriors Arming*, Greek vase VI century B.C. The Metropolitan Museum of Art, Bequest of Joseph H. Durkee, Gift of Darius Ogden Mills, and Gift of Mr. and Mrs. Ruxton Love, by exchange, 1972.

Vincent van Gogh, *Portrait de l'Artiste*, 1886. From the collection of Adelaide Milton de Groot. (Courtesy of the Perls Galleries, N.Y.)

" 'The only questions that really matter ultimately in life are moral ones.' " Thomas P. F. Hoving, in commencement address at Bennington College.

It is true that the tradition of "reciprocal appreciation" dates back to the Impressionists and beyond, but the French have always been, well, *pragmatic* about it. Not long ago, the music critic of a major daily in Paris told me that no French publication paid a critic a living wage. "How can I pan the concert of an impresario who is going to hire me to write his next program notes?" he demanded. So French art critics are often paid by dealers and artists in cash or paintings. Just as food and travel writers feed and travel *gratuit*. (In both cases, it should be added, the French public is not deceived. It *expects* critics to take.)

In Britain and the United States, of course, such venality is unknown. No art publication accepts paid plugs, at least none has been caught at it lately. Using color plates lent by dealers and running a dealer's ad along with a favorable review are regarded as more acceptable, indeed sometimes as essential to survival. Also, I know of no American art critic who has never accepted a token of appreciation from an artist. But the motives are pure.

An old cynic once commented: "The day that I eat in a restaurant and the *maître d'hôtel* tells me he likes my looks so much that my dinner is going to be on the house — on that day I'll believe that people give freebies out of love."

"Some do, some don't," said the artist Robert Motherwell. "If a museum decided to give an artist a huge show, then the artist might very well give a drawing or a wash to the guy who did the work. I really don't think that anybody's buyable. It's completely voluntary. I've had something like fifty museum shows, and never had anybody ask me for something. A couple of times, I've been refused."

Many give, then, and few refuse. Everybody's conscience is positively gleaming. Harold Rosenberg, for example, mounted a *show* of art given him by grateful artists. Greenberg could do as much, if it were his style. Mrs. Burnham writes:

Clem Greenberg, who openly sells these gifts when he needs money, takes a painting with the option that, if he later sees one he likes better, he can trade in the old model. If the artist offers him one he does not like, he rejects it. The late Barnett Newman told Harold Rosenberg of Greenberg's coming into his studio and asking for a painting. Barney was going to give him something small — a lithograph perhaps. "I don't want that," said Greenberg. "I want that big one over there. It's your best picture." And Newman, inwardly raging, capitulated.

Nobody alleges that this influenced Greenberg's writing, in which Geldzahler discerned a "moral grandeur." However, the earnings of a free-lance art critic have got to be small — even if eked out, as Greenberg acknowledged, by a very occasional sale of a painting by an artist whose market value he had much enhanced. But he was not long dependent on such earnings alone. In fact, he was turning away some writing jobs on the ground that he was earning too much already. He was experienced on the business side of the game, having moonlighted for a year at a gallery on Madison Avenue, and he found a way to put his market savvy and his critical eye together. He became adviser to the widow of the artist Morris Louis, and carefully fed his paintings out at steadily rising prices.

When the sculptor David Smith died in 1965, it was fortunate for his two little daughters that Greenberg was around. Smith left 425 pieces and an exclusive selling contract with Marlborough. When that contract expired, Greenberg as executor and business manager negotiated a new one, reducing the gallery's commission from one third to one quarter of the gross. He kept a tight control on sales, not hesitating to turn down a major museum that already, in his opinion, had enough David Smiths. Every few months, he would jack up the prices.

According to the lawyer Ira Lowe, a co-executor, about

half the sculptures had been sold by the end of 1972, and they had yielded the estate about $4,500,000. Lowe said he did not have the figures handy on how much went to the executors, but pointed out that under New York law they could collect up to 15 per cent of the value of an estate, plus fees for special services rendered. Clearly, the executors had done very well for themselves as well as for the heirs.

And David Smith prices were still going up! The sale of *Becca* to the Met at $225,000 didn't hurt. In that deal, it must be said that Greenberg more than earned his fees.

It will be remembered that the sculpture had been featured in Geldzahler's big show in October 1969, which, as Hoving remarked, had enhanced *Becca*'s market value. Now, according to my notes of a telephone conversation with Greenberg, the critic told me: "In late 1969, the asking price was $100,000. At that time, the trustees refused. I told Henry that 'You tell the trustees that the asking price is $125,000.' Then I asked Marlborough to go up to $150,000, and so on."

This agreed with what Hoving and Ira Lowe had earlier recalled, but contradicted Geldzahler, who in a 1973 letter to the *Times* declared that the price for *Becca* had been $250,000 "since late 1969," which would be before or during Henry's show.

Geldzahler was, in fact, contradicting himself. A few weeks before he wrote this letter, he was defending the *Becca* swap in a lecture in Buffalo: "The first year, it was $150,000, and too expensive. Two years later, it was $200,000. Last year, it was $250,000. I got saved, and we bought it in exhange for five or six so-called masterpieces."

Greenberg later called back to deny my report that he had said, "I told Henry to tell the trustees . . ." Instead, he insisted, he must have said, "I told Marlborough . . ."

The point may have some importance, since Greenberg's dual role as an accredited museum adviser to Geldzahler and as business manager of the Smith estate might be construed as a conflict of interest.

Greenberg and Geldzahler shared another kind of interest conflict which, to be fair, is rather common among American critics and curators. Henry also was a collector, and since his arrival in New York in 1960 he had naturally been picking up for himself the work of artists he liked: Warhol, Stella, Kelly, Hans Hofmann. It was only natural that he should feature the same artists in his shows and galleries at the Met, and commend them to such clients as the Stanley Woodwards, who paid him a monthly retainer for the service. It was also natural that as his preferences changed, he would sell, say, a Warhol or a Frank Stella to buy a Hofmann or a Smith.

The dealer André Emmerich, who handled some of Henry's trades, said he was disturbed at any implication of impropriety. "Every museum person I know who has the *means* to collect, *does* so," he told me. "Geldzahler has in no way pioneered this, or done exceptional things. He has not broken any professional rules. The things Henry Geldzahler owns are not of a scale for museum ownership."

True, the enormous paintings of his friends were hung in the Met, not in Henry's duplex. Emmerich acknowledged that the spectacular rise in the prices of these artists had aroused suspicion, but he held as aberrant the British rule that curators may not collect for themselves in the area of their responsibility. "The English attitude," he said, "is puritanical and not very healthy."

One rainy Saturday late in January 1973, I called at Geldzahler's place, in a town house off Washington Square. A youth hung my dripping coat in a closet with a shelf full of Henry's wide-brimmed hats, and led me to a sitting room fitted with freeform beige leather chairs. Henry entered — plump, bearded, smoking a cigar, yet looking like a sad blue-eyed child. His essential likableness came over strongly.

The Met by this time was no longer cooperating with the *Times,* but on the phone Geldzahler had told me, "I have nothing to hide," and had even cut short a trip to the Midwest in order to meet me. He refused, apologetically, to answer only two questions: whose idea had it been to raise money by selling pictures from the de Groot collection, and how much had they fetched? But he talked freely about the swap for the *Becca,* his dislike for the Modigliani and his $60,000 money-back guarantee to Frank Lloyd.

Were you qualified to judge the value of French paintings? "Yes, I follow the market . . . They were pictures that were not, in my opinion, of a quality to hang in my galleries at the Metropolitan. As far as scholars are concerned, the pictures become more valuable somewhere else."

Do you know where they are today?

"No."

Did you go back to Knoedler to see if it would pay the $350,000 it estimated they were worth?

"No, but it was quite clear they were leaving out their profit."

Why not sell them at public auction?

"I suppose that, in retrospect, I'm sorry I didn't. But at the time, it was the trade I was interested in. To me, the *Becca* was the most important piece in the estate and I didn't want it to go elsewhere . . ."

Was there an immediate prospect of its sale?

"No, but I'd been trying to get the sculpture into the collection for three years."

Geldzahler recalled that in 1967, Hoving had promoted

him from associate curator of American art to curator of twentieth-century art, defined as anything by anybody born after 1875. This of course included French paintings, an area he had never shown much interest in. He recalled: "Rorimer asked me at Harvard in 1959 to come to the Metropolitan, and I said no. He was surprised and asked why, and I said because the Metropolitan isn't interested in modern art. He said, 'Come and see me at Christmas, and we'll talk.'"

One might think that putting Henry in charge of the French masters was like setting a fox to guard the henhouse — except that he looked more like a teddy bear. Actually, he said, he and Everett Fahy, the curator of European paintings, had resisted the sale of certain pieces. Asked which ones, he mentioned Picasso's *Woman in White* and *The Coiffure*. (These were among the major pictures that, as Canaday had reported, were on the market in early 1972.) "We cleaned *The Coiffure* and it turned out to be a much better picture than we had suspected," Geldzahler said.

(Colleagues tell an anecdote that puts Henry in a less protective role. During the 1971 drive to raise funds by peddling surplus art, Henry is said to have brought into a curatorial meeting, as a candidate for disposal, the even more famous Picasso harlequin called *The Actor*. Chief Curator Theodore Rousseau stared with disbelief and said: "Not that one! Henry, take it back.")

Henry confided that he had been "terrified" to read my report* that, according to museum records, the funds from cash sales of his de Groot paintings had been applied toward the Velázquez and the Annibale Carracci that Hoving had bought. But he said he had since been assured that

---

* Later confirmed by the Met's "white paper."

the money remained in his department as a credit against future purchases, as he had been promised. Already, he had been allowed to buy out of these funds a Hans Hartung, for $25,000, from the artist's dealer, Jean LeFebre. (It was a price that made other dealers whistle.)

I asked why he did not buy other European modern masters to replace the ones he had sold. "I just don't have the money," he replied. "We should have a Paul Klee, a Mondrian, a Matisse — and we don't. The quality I want would be so expensive — $150,000 to $1,000,000 — that I'd have to go back to general funds, and be turned down."

Then he added another reason.

"The Museum of Modern Art has the most extraordinary collection of European modern masters in the world. I'd prefer to collect in areas where the MOMA is less strong. For example, Art Deco."

Or David Smiths and Diebenkorns . . . If you can't beat MOMA in one field, quit it and try another. This view fits in fairly well with Hoving's policy of "refining and upgrading the collections" by selling art that doesn't make a splash, in order to buy art that does. It may also help the reader to appreciate the full flavor of a visit to the room that Henry fitted at the Met to show off his new *Becca*. There she stands, six gleaming plaques of stainless steel welded together, with Diebenkorn's lined patch on the nearest wall. Each bears the legend "Bequest of Adelaide Milton de Groot." Nearby are a Jackson Pollock, and one of Clement Greenberg's Morris Louis's. And serenely gazing on them all, as if in fond ridicule, is Picasso's motherly *Woman in White*.

CHAPTER 12

Marlborough Country

Every curator is a frustrated art dealer.

— A Madison Avenue dealer, commenting on
transactions of the Metropolitan Museum

Meeting the critic John Canaday on his way to cover an exhibition at the Met, a curator glumly saluted him: "Welcome to Marlborough country."

Actually, not all of the peculiar deals then being uncovered involved the Marlborough galleries — only the most lucrative ones. A few others remained to be looked into.

As I was leaving Ted Rousseau's office in early January 1973, after hearing his explanation of the swap of six French paintings for two pieces from Marlborough, he handed me a promised list of art disposed of by the Met in 1971–72. In studying it, I was surprised to learn that, contrary to the assurance given me by Hoving and Rousseau, at least five valuable paintings from the de Groot collection had been secretly sold, in addition to those already disclosed.

A Renoir, *In the Garden at Cognes*, and a Boudin, *Market in Brittany*, went to the Newhouse Galleries. Ross Newhouse said he had acquired them from the Met in a private auction of dealers on a sealed bid, and had resold them "at what we thought was a fair markup." He would not disclose what he had paid for them — actually, it was $80,000 — nor what he had received for them.

The Met had also sold three outstanding paintings by the late German expressionist Max Beckmann to a relative newcomer to the Madison Avenue scene, Serge Sabarsky. Rousseau explained that there was no market for Beckmanns outside Germany, and Sabarsky was the only dealer around with an interest in them.

The artist's widow, Mathilde Beckmann, and her agent, Catherine Viviano, said the three pictures were "conservatively" worth $190,000. This, I then told them, was precisely double what I had learned that Sabarsky had paid for them.

Miss Viviano, author of a book on Beckmann and the leading specialist in the market, complained: "I never understood why the museum did not call me to inquire about values. I certainly would have considered buying the paintings, or I'd have found them a buyer."

Since artists' widows are notoriously prejudiced about the market values of their husbands' works, I questioned two other New York dealers who buy and handle Beckmanns. Both were angry that they had not been consulted by the Met. Allan Frumkin waived judgment on one of the three Beckmanns, because he had not seen it, but estimated that the other two must be worth more than $150,000. Richard L. Feigen said that, as a private collector, he would have paid at least $155,000 for the three. He added bitterly that Rousseau and other Met people had dined in his home and *seen* his Beckmanns, but hadn't given him a crack at the deal.

(It transpired much later that Curator Henry Geldzahler had appraised the three Beckmanns at $20,000, $18,000 and $12,000, for a total of $50,000. The critic Emily Genauer suggested this had been done to avoid the more stringent procedures required under the bylaws for disposal of items worth $25,000 or more. Incidentally, the Met's white paper said the proceeds had been used "to partially reim-

burse the Fletcher Fund for the purchase of the Velázquez" — flouting the understanding that sales revenues
from any department would be applied to purchases in the
same area, in this case contemporary art.)

But the Beckmanns were relatively small pickings. Fei-
gen recalled having introduced to Chief Curator Rousseau
in late 1971 a collector willing to pay a record price for a
Douanier Rousseau (one had just been sold for $775,000),
but he had been told that Miss de Groot's painting was not
for sale. Months later, the picture was secretly sold to
Marlborough for $600,000, along with a van Gogh for
$850,000. It will be recalled that the Rousseau was re-
portedly sold in Japan for $2,000,000 and that Frank Lloyd
of Marlborough was asking $1,500,000 for the van Gogh.

In percentage terms, Lloyd's profit on the David Smith
swap may have been even greater. This speculation is supported by a curious telephone conversation I had with
Clement Greenberg, the executor and business manager of
the David Smith estate, about two weeks after I had broken
the story of the trade.

"The estate owes you a case of champagne," Greenberg
said.

*Sorry I can't accept, but I'd be glad to split a bottle with
you. How come?*

"We got $250,000, minus 25 per cent commission for
Marlborough . . . There's a lawyer friend of mine here
— can I ask him something? . . . On good advice, I must
content myself to say, we got it."

*Had he been mistaken when he told me he had gotten
$225,000 for the Becca?*

"I told the truth before. Draw your own conclusions."

Evidently, the Marlborough gallery had decided that it
had received more for the David Smith than it had originally reported. By giving the estate an additional $25,000,

it tacitly acknowledged the error. It was also retroactively raising the nominal price of its sale to the Met.

It followed that Marlborough might feel it owed a bonus check to the Metropolitan Museum, as well. Such generosity would only be consistent with the spirit in which the gallery had entered the deal, as recounted to me by Marlborough vice president David McKee:

> For some time, the Metropolitan had been anxious to acquire the *Becca*, one of the key works remaining in the estate. They wanted the Smith and the Diebenkorn, and they didn't have the funds to pay for it, and Marlborough volunteered to help. Whereupon Frank Lloyd looked at those paintings and was interested in acquiring them for an amount equivalent to the Smith and Diebenkorn . . .
>
> From our point of view, it was two separate transactions.

Nevertheless, the gallery had given a bonus to the Smith estate. Had it done the same for the Met? At the gallery, it was said that Frank Lloyd handled all the business side, that the paintings had gone to Zurich or somewhere and nobody here knew anything about it.

At the Met, the information window was slammed shut. This was a direct and unfortunate result of my own published stories about the David Smith swap, the missing *Odalisque* and Miss de Groot's will and trust fund.

The scandal had become an obsession in the art world. Collectors and donors were writing angry letters and seeing their lawyers about changing their wills. The Met was not alone in being affected. In Albany, New York state legislators cut the budget for subsidies to all the arts from $5 million to $2 million, citing the behavior of the Met as one good reason.

Directors of the Association of Art Museum Directors, meeting in New York, privately considered an inquiry into the Met's flouting of their ethical guidelines but decided against it, for reasons they chose not to disclose. Art scholars took a different stand. Directors of the dominant organization in the field, the College Art Association, invited Hoving and Dillon to a closed meeting. Neither showed up, but Vice Director Rousseau and Secretary Ashton Hawkins did. The C.A.A. board heard them out, then adopted what may well be the most severe rebuke ever administered to the trustees of an American cultural institution by the spokesmen for the nation's art scholars.

The resolution disputed Hoving's stand that the trustees owned the art "and hence have no accountability to the public"; voiced concern that "the stated intentions of donors have not been consistently respected"; said that disclosure of the Met's secret disposals had weakened "the confidence of the public and potential donors in other museums"; expressed fear that art leaving the Met would no longer be available to scholars for study; charged that "contradictory public statements and inconsistent administration of professed standards for deaccessioning by the director have not been in the best interests of the museum or his profession"; challenged Hoving's judgments on the value of specific works, and urged the addition of scholars to the board of trustees.

"Whether or not the stewardship of the Trustees has contributed to a financial dominution of the museum's assets might be determined by an appropriate government agency," the resolution said. The state attorney general, Louis J. Lefkowitz, had come to the same conclusion. On the day the art scholars were meeting, he announced an inquiry into the legality and propriety of the Met's deals. He explained:

"We're concerned primarily about whether the works of art that the museum is disposing of, as reported in *The*

New York Times, were held subject to restrictions against such disposition and, if there were no restrictions, whether the sales were provident, prudent and reasonable."

Secretary Ashton Hawkins said the Met "was cooperating fully" with the Lefkowitz probe and called it "perfectly proper" and "not that unusual."

No such prior inquiry into the Met could be recalled, but Hawkins' statement went a long way to undermine Hoving's stand, enunciated the preceding November 29 at New York University, that "every work of art is entirely owned by the trustees."* Hawkins was himself a former assistant to Lefkowitz, and presumably knew that in the last analysis the museum belonged to the public, and that the attorney general was obliged to defend the public interest.

Hoving himself conceded the point in commenting on a bill by Councilman Carter Burden to require any subsidized museum to disclose in advance any selling plans. (Burden explained that during the Hoving regime "deceit and dissimulation have been elevated to the level of official museum policy.") Hoving replied that the Met would be "delighted to study the bill when prepared" and was drafting "a detailed white paper which will discuss the transactions and the recent disposals."

"For 103 years the Metropolitan has existed and thrived in a healthy partnership with the city," he said. "Any intimation that the trustees or the staff of the Metropolitan own the works of art is not intended."

The white paper had been announced in a letter to the *Times* signed by Dillon in behalf of the trustees. Sources in the museum said the letter had been drafted by Hawkins and read to some trustees by telephone. It declared that

---

* Asked about this at a Bar Association forum, Trustee Francis Plimpton observed, "If Tom Hoving said that, he was out of his mind."

"the museum's trustees and its general counsel [Herbert Brownell] believe that the stewardship of the collection is and has been legally and ethically correct and in the best interests of the public," that "many of the recent reports in the press have been incomplete and inaccurate" and that "the museum has volunteered to make no further sales or exchanges for the next ninety days without prior notification to the Attorney General's office."

"Rather than attempt a piecemeal clarification of the questions that have been raised," Dillon concluded, "the museum is preparing a publication outlining its disposal policy with full documentation and photographs of the paintings sold in 1971 and 1972, giving reasons for the sale and what was obtained."

From here on, inquiries about sensitive details of the Met's art dealings were turned away with such statements as, "We can't talk about that while the Attorney General is conducting an inquiry," or, "That will be in the white paper."

Like Dillon's promise a year earlier to make public any decisions to sell art, fulfillment was delayed. The white paper was to appear "shortly," then in a few weeks, which stretched on. A team of administrators and lawyers, drafting, editing and revising, kept running into problems. There were experts who refused to sign statements that certain of the disposed works were inferior or fraudulent. There were comparative prices to be sifted; some of them would support the Met's case, but others would hurt it.

For example, the draft would make much of records showing the low prices obtained at auctions for Beckmanns (to defend the price at which it had sold three), but would ignore the low prices obtained at auction for David Smiths, Diebenkorns and Hans Hartungs, which it had bought. (Actually, contemporary art does badly at auctions except when dealers artificially support prices. For this reason, the work of *living* artists is best sold by canvassing collectors. A prior question here was whether the Met should be selling such art at all.)

The scope of the white paper grew handily. Dillon had said it would cover sales in 1971 and 1972. But when I asked about the El Greco that was sold in 1965, I was first promised the information in a day or so, then stalled for a week, and finally told it would be in the white paper.

(When it finally appeared more than five months later, the white paper contained no documentation and no photographs, contrary to Dillon's promise. Rather, it said in a preface: "The facts set forth below come principally from documents in the Museum's files but were augmented where necessary for completeness by the recollections of Museum officials who participated in the events described." The booklet generally defended the wisdom and propriety of the Met's transactions, but confirmed the revelations of the *Times*. At a news conference, it was put to Roswell Gilpatric, chairman of the special committee of eight trustees, who signed the white paper,[*] that it proved that museum officials had repeatedly lied to the public, and for them to have participated in this investigation was tantamount to Haldeman and Ehrlichman writing the Senate report on Watergate. Gilpatric replied that the inquiry had been thoroughly independent. He implied, however, that there had been no serious effort to question critics or the dealers who had traded with the Met. In answer to

[*] Gilpatric had had some experience at investigations. He was the central figure in the TFX inquiry, which sought to learn why the huge contract for the ill-fated swingwing jet had been denied to Boeing — the low bidder, favored by the Air Force — and awarded to General Dynamics, with which Deputy Defense Secretary Gilpatric's law firm had been involved. Nothing ever came of that investigation, either.

another question, Dillon volunteered that this reporter had been unfair and biased. He did not offer any examples.)

As with Watergate, there was never any real prospect that the full story of the Met's dealings could emerge without a judicial examination of the parties, under oath. Several groups of dealers, collectors and members of the museum had considered filing civil suits against the trustees, demanding an accounting of their stewardship and recovery of any assets that might be found to have been dissipated by negligence and imprudence. Their lawyers had warned them, however, that such a suit would be expensive and difficult against the money and power that Dillon, Hoving and the tax-supported Met would employ in their defense. It was with relief that these citizens suspended their projects on the news that the attorney general would wage the fight for them.

But "the General," as Lefkowitz is called, was in a more delicate position than was widely appreciated. A state official does not seek an all-out fight with such a powerhouse as the board of the Met, closely tied as it is with its honorary trustee Governor Nelson Rockefeller. The General could spare only one young assistant, Palmer Wald, for the inquiry — and only part time. Wald proceeded with due discretion. At the Met, incidentally, he dealt primarily with former Assistant Attorney General Ashton Hawkins, now secretary of the museum.

Wald does not seem to have got anywhere with the Marlborough galleries, if indeed he tried. The attorney general's office had in fact been trying for more than a year to come to grips with that worldwide art enterprise, and had not so much as succeeded in unraveling its corporate structure. Though unrelated to the Met, the case is worth looking at here for the light it sheds on the art market and the elusive personality of Frank Lloyd.

CHAPTER 13

Outsmarting Frank Lloyd

> You must realize how good a negotiator I am . . . I feel I completely outnegotiated Mr. Lloyd on everything.
>
> — The Honorable Frank E. Karelsen, Sr., reporting to executors of the Mark Rothko estate

> The trouble with you Americans is, you believe in bourgeois honesty.
>
> — Remark attributed to Frank Lloyd

Mark Rothko detested the art market. He told his friend Jacob Kainen that "this commercial racket" was "demeaning" to an artist. "No more dealers, no more shows," he said. "I can live well enough by selling a few paintings a year." A few months later, in February 1970, he committed suicide. He was sixty-six years old.

"I have a hunch," wrote John Fischer in *Harper's*, "that at least a contributing cause was his long anger: the justified anger of a man who felt destined to paint temples, only to find his canvases treated as trade goods."

Success came too late for Rothko. He had sacrificed his youth and middle years to Art — like Chaim Soutine, Marc Chagall and others from the ghettos of East Europe.

In that stinking Parisian beehive of genius called *la Ruche*, a circular tenement infected with the odors of the toilet in the court and the horse slaughterhouse of Vaugirard, it is related that the famished and half-mad Soutine agonized before his easel one day, staring at a herring he had somehow obtained for a still-life and fighting the temptation to eat it first, when a rat seized it before his eyes. What would a collector pay for that still-life today?

Chagall survived to enjoy a happy and productive old age, basking in adoration and opulence. But he could not forget. When collectors begged him, as they often did, to sign some of his early oils and lithographs they had picked up for a song, he angrily refused; why should he, with a stroke of the pen, add more value to a work than he could get for a hundred such during his hungry years?

Just so in New York, Rothko recalled going from museum to museum not long ago, offering two of his paintings for $300 that he badly needed. They all turned him down. Later, in the art market boom of the nineteen sixties — when he, too, was entering his sixties — those museums were willing to pay tens of thousands of dollars for one of those paintings. But the sweet smell of success stank in his nostrils. "I hate art," Rothko said.

Like other pioneers of abstract expressionism, once its market was well established, Rothko was persuaded to switch from the Sidney Janis Gallery to Marlborough, a growing international financial art enterprise headed by another East European émigré, Frank Lloyd.

The New York branch, then called Marlborough-Gerson, had no history of service to living artists there, but it did have business savvy and powerful financial connections on both sides of the Atlantic. Soon Marlborough became the dominant representative of successful members of the New York School: David Smith, Ad Reinhardt, Robert Motherwell, Rothko. Motherwell explained to me that Marlborough had unequaled ability to tap the burgeoning corporate market for art. Who else could have sold a David Smith to Pepsico for $150,000? Or another to the Metropolitan Museum for $225,000? Then there were its

European connections. Ralph J. Colin, general counsel to the New York gallery, told me: "Marlborough is almost unique in its ability to make a world market and to get museums to put on shows that look like museum shows but are in fact Marlborough shows."

By 1969, the year before his suicide, Rothko was free of all concern with dealers and shows, and all the detestable fakery that surrounded art. That year he sold Marlborough 105 paintings for $1,446,000, and gave it exclusive rights to handle any paintings he might sell in the next eight years. In return, he demanded and obtained the right to "put" — that is, sell — four pictures of his own choice each year to Marlborough at 90 per cent of the going retail value. This meant a virtually assured annual income in six figures; Rothko was not fantasizing when he told Kainen he could live by selling a few paintings a year and was pulling out of the commercial racket — "no more dealers, no more shows."

In these dealings, Rothko enjoyed the counsel of his seventy-seven-year-old friend and accountant, Bernard J. Reis, who was also accountant to Marlborough. Though he was not a lawyer, Reis even drew up Rothko's will. In the end, Rothko did not have much better luck with his will than Adelaide Milton de Groot did with hers.

Inexplicably ignoring his wife and their two children — who later applied for and obtained the statutory 50 percent — the artist left his fortune to a Mark Rothko Foundation. He wanted it to help not young but elderly struggling artists, an original and revealing idea. But he left the details to his friends and executors: Reis, the artist Theodore Stamos, and Morton Levine, an anthropologist.

When Rothko died on February 25, 1970, he left 798 paintings covering the range of his life's work and worth, by any accounting, many millions of dollars. His three friends wasted no time in disposing of them: two months to probate the will, three weeks more to negotiate the sale and consignment of the paintings to Marlborough. As revealed by the litigation that followed, the sequence of events in these twelve weeks is remarkable.

According to court papers, Reis and Stamos appear to have turned Rothko's studio over to Marlborough in March, lock, stock and lease. Marlborough's staff then began going over the paintings to choose 100 for a Rothko memorial exhibition that would open at the Venice Biennale that summer and then tour Europe.

In April, Reis moved into Marlborough as secretary-treasurer. He insisted that this appointment had been made in January and with Rothko's knowledge, but he was uneasy enough about it to have written a memorandum to his fellow executors dated April 30, saying: "Because of my professional connection with Marlborough–New York I do not want to participate in the negotiations, but do want to approve any contract relating to the disposition of the paintings. I shall assist with all my background, knowledge and experience."

Levine, the anthropologist, was still worried about the dual role of Reis and could not understand the need for haste in disposing of the Rothko paintings. Also, he testified later, he wanted the contract submitted to the surrogate's court for approval. He said he was told — erroneously — that the surrogate would have declined jurisdiction, and any delay would doom the planned Biennale exhibition, which was expected to enhance greatly the value of the estate. Levine bowed to the superior experience of his co-executors. He was not aware, he said, that Stamos was then negotiating a contract with Marlborough for his own work — at better terms, incidentally, than those given the late Mark Rothko.

To negotiate with Frank Lloyd, the estate hired Frank E. Karelsen, Sr., a seventy-eight-year-old member of the New York Establishment who had long been president of the Board of Education. They met at Marlborough on May 19, and Karelsen came out like the cat that swallowed the canary. "You must realize how good a negotiator I am," the old man told the executors. ". . . I feel I completely outnegotiated Mr. Lloyd on everything."

For the 100 paintings going to the Biennale — the pick of the lot — Karelsen said he had asked $3,000,000 and Lloyd had offered $1,000,000. They settled on $1,800,000, to be paid by the Liechtenstein section of Lloyd's network, Marlborough AG, over a period of twelve years without interest. (Discounting for what amounted to an interest-free loan, the effective price of the 100 paintings was computed to be $1,204,809, or an average of $12,048.09 each. This does not take into account the enormous depreciation in the buying power of the dollar to be anticipated over the next twelve years.)

Karelsen consigned the remaining 698 paintings to Marlborough–New York as exclusive selling agent, with the gallery in effect setting prices and taking a 50 per cent commission — except when it enlisted another gallery in the sale, whereupon the commission might be higher.

Rothko's widow died the same year. The sculptor Herbert Ferber, guardian of the Rothkos' daughter, Kate, was not able to obtain a copy of the contracts until a year later. In her behalf, he then filed suit charging a conspiracy to defraud the estate and asking that the executors be replaced and the contracts nullified. Attorney General Lefkowitz soon joined the suit in behalf of the future beneficiaries of the Mark Rothko Foundation.

The petition was opposed by Marlborough, Reis, Stamos and the Rothko Foundation, which for the most part they seem to have controlled. Levine got his own lawyer and, in effect, turned state's evidence.

The defendants argued that the deal was sound and fair because, among other things, Marlborough was the only possible market, since Rothko had signed a contract in 1970 that barred any other gallery from selling his output for eight years.

The judge, Surrogate Millard L. Midonick, expressed doubt that this contract extended after the artist's death, since it was based on Rothko's selling to the gallery four pictures a year of his choice, at 90 per cent of the retail price. His earlier deal with Marlborough, incidentally, gave the gallery a commission of 33⅓ per cent, as opposed to the 50 per cent and more it was claiming on the 698 paintings in the estate.

The record does not show what commission Stamos granted the gallery, but he did get an advance drawing account against sales and the right of approval over prices of his works. (It may be noted that, in negotiating for the David Smith estate, Clement Greenberg cut Marlborough's commission to 25 per cent and set the prices himself. It was still a good deal for Marlborough.)

Surrogate Midonick chided the defense for not having submitted the contract to the court before signing it — precisely what Levine had suggested. Then he issued an injunction barring further sales of Rothko paintings without such prior approval, pending a trial.

"The appearance of self-dealing is so strong in this case that the court could not permit performance under the contract," he said.

The court pointed out that it could be difficult to collect damages from Marlborough AG, a Liechtenstein corporation. It was in fact impossible to obtain any information from it at all; Marlborough's lawyers argued that under the corporation laws of Liechtenstein, it would be a criminal offense to divulge anything.

Reis said he had lost most of his Rothko records in moving out of his accounting offices. But from some estate papers and sketchy pretrial examinations, the plaintiffs were able to pick up some clues. In an affidavit, they told the court that the New York gallery had resold seventeen of the paintings first bought by the Liechtenstein affiliate, and that the seventeen went for $1,264,000 — more than the effective price that the estate got for all 100. The resale figures ranged from $48,000 to $180,000 — from four to fifteen times the average price received by the estate.

Two more documents covered the sale of thirteen paintings from among the 698 that had been consigned to Marlborough–New York. They were placed through another gallery, and the estate was advised that the lot had fetched $620,000, from which the two galleries took commissions totaling $372,000. But after Kate Rothko's guardian began asking questions, so the papers indicate, a revised statement was submitted. This one mysteriously eliminated the second gallery and its commission, and put the price of the thirteen pictures at $535,000. So instead of $248,000 the estate got $267,500.

(This incident strangely parallels the affair of the David Smith *Becca*, sold to the Met at a given price of $225,000. It will be recalled that after that deal came under public scrutiny, Marlborough quietly gave the Smith estate a new statement, listing the price at $250,000.)

The plaintiffs found that whole lots of Rothkos had been sold to galleries where one would hardly expect to shop for abstract expressionists. For example, twenty-nine went to William Hallsborough Ltd. of London, which does not advertise in the weekly listing of the Sunday *Times* but is registered in a directory of galleries as selling old masters.

On what evidence they had, the plaintiffs figured that the estate had been done out of something like $10 million so far. But when they tried to trace the path of other paintings already sold, they hit a stone wall. The attorney general and Edward J. Ross, Kate's lawyer, could not even establish who owned Marlborough. The New York gallery was chartered as a privately held corporation, with Reis, David McKee and Pierre Levai, a nephew of Lloyd's, as directors. (Levai's wife was assistant to Theodore Rousseau at the Metropolitan Museum, which caused some grumbling among galleries less favored with the Met's business.)

The president's office was left vacant. Lloyd, generally regarded as its boss, held no formal post; he was an "adviser," Vice President McKee told me. McKee would not say who held the controlling stock interest, nor what were the relations between Marlborough of New York and Marlborough of Liechtenstein — not to mention the Marlboroughs in London, Zurich, Rome, Toronto, Montreal and Tokyo.

Lloyd himself was of course capable of giving the answers, but a series of investigators had sounded him on the subject with only ironic results. He told David Shirey of the *Times* that the Marlborough galleries were independently controlled by a family trust, of which he was only an "adviser." "I don't have any money in my pocket," he said. "I have to depend on my family for everything I get."

The family is apparently generous. A natty, tough little man of sixty-two with a Viennese accent, a receding hairline and a permanent tan, Lloyd had acquired a young blond wife, a villa on the Riviera, apartments in Paris and New York and an estate in the Bahamas. The last afforded him part-time relaxation and year-round immunity from income tax, if, as it was said, he had indeed become a

Bahamian citizen. (The bookkeeping for the Marlborough network is cleared through Liechtenstein, where many of the major deals are registered. "There's a tax advantage to it, I hear," Lloyd told Shirey.)

Lloyd likes to say he was in oils in his native Austria, where he owned a chain of service stations. He fled as a refugee to France, then Britain, during the war, joined the army and, it is said, accumulated a modest stake as a camp cook. The base of his future prosperity, though, was a collection of old books and manuscripts owned by a fellow refugee, Harry Fischer. In peacetime, the two opened the first Marlborough gallery in London.

Those were years when an alert operator could make a quick fortune picking up art in devastated Europe. Lloyd rapidly acquired such financial backers and clients as the industrialists Bruno Haftel of Argentina, Giovanni Agnelli of Italy, Assis Chateaubriand of Brazil and the Rothschilds of Paris (who underwrote his purchase of the Rothko paintings). He also hired representatives like David Somerset, the future Duke of Beaufort, to give the gallery "some class."

Lloyd's technique in building new branches was to go into partnership with an existing gallery and eventually buy out the former owner. (Fischer went away mad.) In New York, it was the Gerson gallery, which became Marlborough-Gerson, then Marlborough. "It was a fat cat among the pigeons," said Jill Kornblee, another dealer.

Ralph Colin, Lloyd's New York lawyer, has described his empire in relation to the rest of the art trade as "U.S. Steel in a community of blacksmiths." It is a felicitous analogy to the modern business experience, where each year many thousands of entrepreneurs try their chances, the vast majority fail, and the few winners are bought out by the giants.

Less successful competitors complained that Marlborough never discovered a new talent; it just bought out those that had arrived, offering substantial drawing accounts and solid market connections with the interlocking worlds of finance, high society and museums. According to Shirey, Lloyd won Adolph Gottlieb with a one-man show; helped seduce David Smith by finding him a pair of size twelve, triple-E shoes, and was a lavish host to many others. One way or another, he acquired Henry Moore, Jacques Lipchitz, Mark Rothko, Larry Rivers, Robert Motherwell. And having a monopoly on these names meant that the clientele for important modern art had to come to Lloyd. After a visit to Rome, Lloyd could say, "I have put the Pope on my private list."

Even better than owning artists was owning their estates. · The *Wall Street Journal* said of Lloyd: "With typical lack of sentimentality, he defines an 'important' artist as a dead artist — the longer dead, the more important." Lloyd acquired rights to the estates of Jackson Pollock, Ad Reinhardt, Kurt Schwitters, David Smith and Mark Rothko, among others.

Pollock's widow, Lee Krasner, is a Marlborough artist who has little sympathy for the complaints of rival dealers. She told Shirey: "All those horses' asses in the art world envy Lloyd. They yak about quality and purity, but what they do in the name of quality and purity is not to be believed . . . Lloyd has done alone what they couldn't do all together."

Robert Motherwell, who finally pulled out, was less enthusiastic. He called Marlborough "a cold, monstrous situation."

"I once asked them for a loan, and somebody there told me I'd be rich when I'm dead," he said. "Marlborough always wants to handle art on its own terms, not the artist's. They want to dictate when to show and where.

And they accept only senior artists. They've never promoted anyone young. In fact, they prefer to handle estates."

"I don't give a damn what anybody says," Lloyd observed. "There's only one measure of success in running a gallery: making money. Any dealer who says it's not is a hypocrite or will soon be closing his doors."

This, then, was the man whom Frank Karelsen outnegotiated in May 1970, and whom Thomas P. F. Hoving outnegotiated two years later. Hoving had, to be sure, long experience at outsmarting foxy dealers, such as Ante Topic-Mimara and Julius H. Weitzner . . .

CHAPTER 14

Outsmarting Weitzner

> This type of exchange is the very exemplar of the
> museum's policy of refinement.
>
> — Thomas Hoving

Seldom has the loser in a horse trade been so sporting about it as Julius H. Weitzner. True, he said, the boys at the Met never told him that the nag had the blind staggers. But he had no hard feelings. "I don't know why you fellows are after Mr. Hoving," the dealer told me. "He's 100 per cent straight."

To be sure, Weitzner was not actually out of pocket on the swap. "*You* should make that much every two years," he said.

With one side happy and the other philosophic, the deal would never have drawn attention but for the scandal about other secret art transactions by the Met. Then a rumor began circulating on Madison Avenue that Weitzner had been asking $220,000 for an old master he had obtained from the museum in exchange for one worth perhaps $20,000.

A list of art deals reluctantly surrendered by the museum in early 1973 revealed that more than a year earlier, it had given Weitzner *A Street in Delft* by Jan van der Heyden in exchange for *Community of the Blessed Adoring the Holy Trinity* by Carlo Saraceni, a lesser-known master of the Italian Renaissance.

A van der Heyden in good condition could well go for

$220,000 or more, while auction records suggested that
$20,000 might be a record price for a Saraceni. The most
recent public sale of one was at Sotheby's on July 19, 1969,
when the Earl of Harewood was unloading his collection
to meet estate taxes. On that day, a Saraceni called *Paradise
with the Trinity* went for $1152.

Now in the arcane code of Sotheby, known to all
bidders, a painting listed with only the surname of the artist
is, as the catalogue warns, "in our opinion a work of the
school or by one of the followers of the artist or in his style
and of uncertain date." (The catalogue, incidentally, was
code-named ORCHID. It is a vulgar error to believe that
there is no sentiment in the art business.) With such an
attribution, the price paid seemed to have no bearing on the
value of the Met's Carlo Saraceni. But the description of
the painting was troubling. In what seemed likely to be a
wasted effort, I sent to London for a picture of the Earl of
Harewood's painting and to the museum's public relations
department for one of theirs.

To my astonishment, the two photographs were the
same, except that the London picture was darker and flaky
in one corner. Experts who compared them said they were
probably the same painting, photographed before and after
cleaning and possibly a touch of restoration.

It hardly seemed credible, nevertheless, that the museum
had exchanged a van der Heyden for a $1152 picture of
doubtful attribution. Everett Fahy, the curator of European paintings, was not answering any calls from me since
my inquiry about the missing Ingres *Odalisque*, but
through a mutual acquaintance I conveyed to him an
urgent invitation to examine the two pictures in my office,
since he would not receive me at the Met. He hesitated,
then declined. Minutes later, Theodore Rousseau called
and invited me to bring my photographs to his office.

Hoving, Rousseau and an assistant greeted me. The director held a legal pad in his hand and wrote down each question, withdrawing frequently to confer with Rousseau. He explained that previous interviews "did not lead to accuracy."

The upshot was that, yes, the Saraceni bought by Weitzner in London for $1152 was the Saraceni that was hanging in the Venetian gallery of the Met. And the museum had known it all the time.

As for the van der Heyden, Hoving said:

"Its condition, after examination by the curator and his assistant and the conservator, was described as poor. This picture could never be exhibited in the galleries of the Metropolitan Museum, because it's extremely poorly preserved. Its condition is so deteriorated that it would never be worth trying to restore it. The valuation, I believe, was $14,000."

Continuing at dictation speed, Hoving said:

"To sum up: We feel that we've brought a picture unique to our collection and of major importance, historically and in beauty, in exchange for a deteriorated work, not reparable, of a master whose works we have well represented. This type of exchange is the very example of the museum's policy of refinement, under part of which you stabilize the growth of the collection in numbers, and obtain something superior in quality."

Next day, Hoving telephoned to say that in my story on how Weitzner had parlayed $1152 to something in six figures, I had quoted him correctly. But, he added, "You didn't ask the right questions."

What were the right questions?

"You'll find out."

That mystery cleared itself up in a matter of hours. Two dealers, Clyde Newhouse and Eugene V. Thaw, came forward to say that they had been consulted by Fahy about the van der Heyden before the swap, and both had found it in awful shape. Newhouse opined, however, that, considering that the painting was a genuine van der Heyden which could be sold as "from the collection of the Metropolitan Museum," Hoving's valuation of $14,000 "certainly was low." Thaw, on the other hand, considered the painting as commercially worthless.

"It's the first instance in the whole mess where the museum was right, up to a point," Thaw said. "But the Metropolitan provenance puts a stamp on it. It should have been given to some university collection for study. Putting that sort of thing into circulation is questionable."

In a letter to the *Times* dated the day of these conversations, Hoving added what he had not told me or, it appeared, Weitzner: that doubts had been recorded as to the authenticity of the van der Heyden since at least 1954, and as to its condition since 1947.

So after more than fifty years in the art trade, Weitzner had been stuck on a bad one. This was surprising, in view of his legendary eye for unsuspected values in old masters. As early as 1930, he had made the public prints by buying at a New York auction for $55 a little panel that turned out to be a Rubens. Many such coups followed. The most famous one was in 1968, when Weitzner picked up for $6480 at a country auction in England a painting he identified as a Duccio, and sold to the National Gallery in London seven months later for $360,000.

In Commons, a Tory member charged that this was a typical operation of the notorious London auction ring. This is an informal club of dealers who name one of their number to bid for a desirable item, then meet privately afterward and hold a private auction among themselves, splitting the profit. The M.P. said Weitzner was the kingpin of the ring and should be deported back to his native New York. The Board of Trade announced an inquiry, but Weitzner denied any role in such a ring, and the case was dropped for lack of witnesses.

The $1152 Saraceni was a more modest find. As was his wont, Weitzner took it to his town house off Berkeley Square and cleaned it with his own hand. The colors flamed into brilliance. He called his friend Benedict Nicolson, the learned editor of *The Burlington Magazine*, who was enthusiastic and wrote it up, with permission, in an early issue. This publication, with a color photograph lent by Weitzner (although, as he told me, he was "allergic to getting free publicity"), was cited by Curator Fahy in his application to the Metropolitan trustees for permission to buy the Saraceni. Since the swap cost no money, there was no objection. It should be added that independent scholars agree that the Saraceni is authentic and filled a blank in the museum's collection.

Advised by a transatlantic telephone call that several New York dealers had termed the van der Heyden virtually worthless, Weitzner retorted: "If there's any reflection, it would be on their stupidity." He said he had sold the painting "in the trade."

How had he made out on the deal?

"I did very well. You should make that every two years."

Weitzner told me he was coming to New York to see his tax lawyer and attend an auction of old masters from the Metropolitan Museum, and amiably agreed to sit for his profile. He received me in the book-lined office of what used to be his own gallery on Madison Avenue, hard by Sotheby Parke Bernet. A tall, stooped, white-haired man in banker's gray, wearing a blue polka-dot bowtie and horn-rimmed glasses, he bore his seventy-seven years well.

"I've always been a discoverer of pictures," he said. "I started with six dollars and a pregnant wife." This was on a year-long honeymoon in Paris in 1924, when he said he picked up for six dollars "a beautiful Boudin" at the municipal auction gallery, the Hotel Drouot. He had been a chemist and a professional violinist and then built "a nice import business," but gave it all up to pursue art.

Moral standards were different then, he observed. On his return from Paris, the Customs gave him a hard time because of a nude in a catalogue of pictures from the Louvre. He recalled a Mary Cassatt, one of several pictures he bought from the Rhode Island School of Design. It was a portrait of a woman and two daughters. "Squibb wanted it for a calendar, so they painted a wedding ring on the mother's hand."

Most of Weitzner's greatest exploits involved museums. He is widely credited with having led the swarm of dealers to the honeypot at the Minneapolis Institute of Arts in the mid fifties, but he modestly insisted that he came in only at the end. "Dickie" Davis, the director, had persuaded his tightfisted trustees to buy two fine and costly Impressionists, a Cézanne and a Poussin, by selling a lot of dusty old canvases. "I was silly," Weitzner said. "I didn't go immediately to Minneapolis, I only came in at the very end of it . . . I got about fifty — they were some beautiful pictures. The only picture I didn't get, I offered too much for. It was a Titian. I offered $30,000, and they got scared and pulled it back. If I'd offered $1500, I'd have got it."

Deadpan, Weitzner added that after it was all over he had received a thank-you letter from Davis, saying that, "due to your munificent buying," the Minneapolis Institute had acquired two fine Impressionists.

Even at so sophisticated an institution as the Metropolitan Museum, he said, "some valuable things slip through." It was he who, during the same epoch as the Minneapolis coup, bought a masterwork by Nicholas Manuel Deutsch at an auction of storeroom junk sponsored by Director Rorimer and Curator Rousseau.

"Their great restorer had called it a fake," Weitzner said. "It was appraised by Parke Bernet at $150. Professor [Julius] Held was the only one who recognized it. He told another dealer. I bought it for $6500. I gave it away, for $25,000, to a Swiss museum . . .

"They have an *abondance de richesse* up there. To them, it's crap, but a dealer can find some place where it's good crap."

The van der Heyden, it developed, was "good crap." Weitzner said he'd long had an eye on that painting and had even struck a deal for it twelve years earlier, but it fell through. This, he explained, was the doing of the late Robert Lehman, then vice president of the museum. "My friend Lehman said, 'Let's investigate this a little more; this Weitzner is too smart.' "

The dealer said he had just written the Met a letter, saying he thought he'd been stuck.

"They didn't tell me they had tried to strip the picture in the twenties," he said.

Stripping is the removal of overpainting applied to a picture down through the centuries to get at the original underneath. Apparently, the painting had been found to be beyond repair.

But, Weitzner continued, "they didn't get down to the basic original."

"I had a hunch . . . I can carry the experiment to the point of disintegration. I said, maybe——[a restorer] can pull this thing together. She declined. I begged her, 'Pull this together.' "

(This woman was so alarmed when I called her that I did

not press her on the subject, nor did I mention her name. But another restorer, Mario Modestini, said he had seen the painting in her New York studio, in the final stage of a really major overpainting. "It was very much redone," he said. "Nicely, of course. You have to be an expert to see those things.")

"I never buy any sure pictures," Weitzner said. "It has to have the element of risk in it."

The Dutch painting emerged from restoration "not worthy of the Metropolitan," he acknowledged, but still "worth six figures." Even after splitting with any other dealers involved, he indicated that his profit on the Saraceni–van der Heyden parlay exceeded two years of a reporter's salary, which he estimated at $25,000 a year.

So the museum came out ahead, and the dealer came out ahead. The Earl of Harewood may be considered a loser, but the less he got for his paintings, the less he had to pay in estate tax. And the ultimate buyer of the van der Heyden got — for "six figures" — a more or less genuine Dutch master from the collection of the Metropolitan Museum of Art.

All in all, as Hoving said, an "exemplar" of a museum deal.

CHAPTER 15

The Loot in the Basement

I think that this country more than any other has a
special claim to the arts of all mankind.

— André Emmerich, New York dealer, in
a talk on the illegal art traffic*

Every American museum that collects ancient art is, or was
until recently, a knowing receiver of stolen goods. The
antiquities collection of the greatest of them all, the Metropolitan Museum of Art, was in fact founded on loot. As its
published history recounts without shame, its first director,
General Luigi Palma di Cesnola, more or less illegally dug
up 35,000 art objects on the island of Cyprus while he was
United States consul there after the Civil War and
smuggled them out of the country in defiance of a Turkish
ban. Outbidding the Hermitage and the Louvre, the
founders of the Met bought the collection — or, rather,
most of it, since a portion was lost at sea — for $60,000,
and with it acquired the services of Cesnola. Nearly a
century later, with another flamboyant director at the
helm, the Met was in the hassle of its life over a single item
of suspect origin.

That any ethical question should be raised at all is a
reflection of revolutionary changes that are still under way.
The looting of art is doubtless nearly as ancient as art
itself, but archaeology is not much more than a century

* Quoted by Karl E. Meyer in *The Plundered Past* (Atheneum, 1973).

old, and its explosion into a true scientific discipline with all the tools of modern technology may be said to have begun only after World War II. At the same time, the spectacular boom in art prices and in the collection of primitive and ancient artifacts has given rise to pillage on an industrial scale. Thousands of peasants eke out their livelihood from it; hundreds of dealers and corrupt officials make fortunes from it. The passionate and underpaid devotees of archaeology watch aghast while the history of antiquity disintegrates before their eyes.

The effort to block the illicit traffic was late getting under way. It was helped, as usual, by a scandal. In 1963, the Dumbarton Oaks museum, a dependency of Harvard University, bought a hoard of Byzantine silverwork that could only, it was generally agreed, have come from a clandestine dig in Turkey. Stung by press reports that a great treasure had been permitted to slip out of the country, the Turkish Government barred archaeologists affiliated with Dumbarton Oaks from further excavation there. The ironic threat that scholars should be punished for the deeds of their enemies spurred a budding movement for international action to end the illegal traffic in art.

The old guard among museum trustees, directors and curators was not persuaded. Their arguments ranged from the brutal one that only the United States could *appreciate* this art, to the more sophisticated one that the traffic was going to go on anyhow and any institution that abstained from the market was simply depriving its clientele of beautiful things that would go elsewhere. If they acknowledged that archaeological sites were being damaged and art scattered to the winds without a record of its origin, the old-guard group countered with what may be called the Elgin Marbles defense: the poor countries neither appreciate nor protect their treasures. This often-heard argument is tantamount to saying that if a householder fails to lock his door, it's permissible to rob him. Sadly, there is truth in the complaint about security in the poor countries; the solution might seem to be to help them rather than loot them. Not that we don't give generously at times, but at a UNESCO meeting in Paris not long ago I watched the representatives of the rich countries defeat a 1 per cent surcharge on their dues to be used to protect antiquities. It would have come to less than half a million dollars a year.

The passion for collecting dies hard. Norton Simon, who has his own great museum near Los Angeles, confirmed without embarrassment recently that he had paid $1 million for a bronze god that the Indian Government says was stolen from a temple and smuggled out of India.

"Hell, yes, it was smuggled," the *Times* quoted Simon as saying, "I spent between $15 million and $16 million over the last two years on Asian art, and most of it was smuggled. I don't know whether it was stolen."

Later, Simon said he had been misquoted. He agreed that looting was "terribly destructive" and said the countries concerned should enforce their own laws. The United States should not allow the import of art without clearance from the country of origin. Nonetheless, he indicated he would keep his bronze.

The year 1970 was one of major progress in the fight against the illicit art traffic. First, the University Museum of the University of Pennsylvania, a hotbed of field or "dirt" archaeology, adopted what became known as the Pennsylvania Declaration, pledging never again to buy objects of uncertain origin — that is, stolen art. The Harvard museums followed.* A conference of the Interna-

* Douglas Dillon, president of the Met, was chairman of the Harvard Board of Overseers.

tional Council of Museums met in Paris on what the American delegate, Thomas P. F. Hoving of the Metropolitan, called "the most serious issue facing the museum profession." It adopted a code of ethics holding that "no acquisition should be made without full documentation," and "if a museum is offered objects, the licit quality of which it has reason to doubt, it will contact the competent authorities of the country of origin in an effort to help this country safeguard its national heritage."* The same year, UNESCO adopted an international convention to the same effect, which was later ratified by the United States Senate.

Now 1970 was also the centennial year of the Metropolitan and the Boston Museum of Fine Arts. For the Boston museum and its dynamic director, Perry T. Rathbone, the occasion could not be lost to outdo its New York rival in the acquisitions to be displayed. Rathbone's ambition was his undoing. First, he had allowed his curator of classical art, Cornelius Clarkson Vermeule III, to buy a hoard of 137 gold objects fashioned in the Early Bronze Age from the same dealer who had sold Dumbarton Oaks its Byzantine treasure. Then in Italy, Rathbone had picked up from "a private collector" a little Raphael for a price reported at $600,000. Scandal broke out when the Italian Government proved that the painting had been smuggled out in violation of its laws on are export. It was compounded when it was learned that the picture had entered the United States in a curator's suitcase, undeclared — a fairly pointless oversight in view of the fact that there would be no import duty anyhow. The Boston trustees handed the picture over to Italy and retired Rathbone. (Vermeule became acting director.) To date, they have not got back their money —

---

* Had this code of ethics been effective and enforced in 1963, Hoving could not have acquired the so-called Bury St. Edmunds Cross.

nor the public's money, since the gift was tax deductible. The irony of the affair was amplified when scholars found that the Raphael had been heavily overpainted and was quite possibly a fake.

Meanwhile, the Turkish Government filed a claim to the gold hoard. Boston held on to it, but the publicity was unpleasant. The art critic of the Boston *Globe*, Robert Taylor, complained that while the Boston Museum was getting its lumps, the Metropolitan was hiding in its basement an even richer treasure snitched from the Hermus River Valley in Turkey.

The Turks fired a query to the New York museum. Hoving was off yachting; his second in command, Theodore Rousseau, told the *Times*, "Certainly we have not imported anything illegally from Turkey," and added that the Boston report "seemed to be hearsay fabricated around something that might have a kernel of truth to it." Nobody seems to have pressed him further.

There were in fact 219 kernels. In 1966, the museum had bought a treasure of gold, silver, bronze and earthenware objects and wall paintings for $500,000 from the wealthy New York dealer J. J. Klejman,* who said he had acquired it earlier that year from "ignorant" itinerant traders in Europe. He said the collection had been mixed with "junk" and was bought in at least two different European cities, but insisted rather contradictorily that he had made a sacrifice to scholarship by selling the lot as a whole, instead of breaking it up. Scholars who saw it identified the treasure as from ancient Lydia, the kingdom of Croesus, and said it represented the contents of four 2500-year-old tombs looted near Sardis — where Har-

---

* In 1972, Klejman sold the Newark Museum for $6000 a Roman mosaic that turned out to have been stolen from a museum in Syria. Klejman gave back the money, and the mosaic was returned to Syria.

vard's Fogg Museum, incidentally, was conducting a legitimate dig.

The hoard sat intact in the basement of the museum, shown by Curator Dietrich von Bothmer only to a few favored visitors. But he and Hoving could not resist the temptation to put a pitcher and four other enchanting silver vessels into the centennial show, *Fifty Centuries of Masterpieces.* They were labeled simply, and misleadingly, "Greek." Then they went back into the basement.

The public never made a connection between the *Masterpieces* show and the Boston *Globe* story of looted treasure. But within the Metropolitan Museum, a memorandum about it was being circulated. It had been addressed to President Dillon, Director Hoving, Rousseau, von Bothmer and other colleagues and came from Dr. Oscar White Muscarella, associate curator of ancient Near Eastern art, who was one of the dwindling, increasingly unhappy little band of "dirt archaeologists" at the Met. The memo was a passionate appeal against the destruction of burial mounds, those "time capsules of history," and against the purchase and display of objects lacking a scientific provenance — and often counterfeit, to boot. (In his many research publications, Muscarella had exposed a number of forgeries; like others in the field he was exercised by the fact that museums were showing hundreds of undetected ones and students were using them as examples for comparison.)

In passing, Muscarella warned that if the museum were to show certain objects in its possession, it might trigger "drastic action" against Western archaeologists in the Near East. And in a postscript, the curator said a State Department official had called him that morning to arrange for a Turkish journalist to look at the objects from Turkey in the basement. Muscarella had replied, he said, that his department had no such objects — which was literally true, since the Lydian hoard belonged to von Bothmer's Greek and Roman department.

(Muscarella's loyalty was ill rewarded. Half a year earlier, he had responded to Dillon's invitation to the staff to address any grievances to him. He wrote a long letter decrying the wretched professional and economic status of the curators — as a seasoned and much-published archaeologist, he was getting $11,500 a year — and he begged that the staff be granted academic freedom and a voice in policy similar to those accorded most university faculties. Dillon passed the letter to Hoving, who was not pleased. Ultimately, Muscarella was dismissed three times. Unlike a score of others who resigned by request or were laid off, he stayed on through a civil suit. In a pending complaint, the National Labor Relations Board charges that he and many others were penalized to discourage their organization of a staff association.)

Dillon sent Muscarella a note congratulating him on his contribution to the *Masterpiece* show and promising substantial action on the problem posed by the UNESCO treaty on the trade in stolen art. In their private discussions, trustees and administrators expressed concern about the handicaps that the treaty might impose on the museum's mission of acquisition.

But the minutes of the trustees' meeting on March 14, 1972, disclose that General Counsel Herbert Brownell had explained "reservations and understandings" in the treaty that "would adequately protect the interests of the Museum." So, "there being no objection . . . it was the sense of the meeting that the Trustees of the Metropolitan Museum of Art favor the UNESCO Convention in the form presented to the Senate last month."

At this very time, the Metropolitan Museum learned of the existence of a hitherto unknown Euphronios vase.

CHAPTER 16

The Calyx Krater

There is a line in a poem by James Elroy Flecker, "Broken vases widowed of their wine . . ." I've often thought of that in this affair.

— Dietrich von Bothmer to the author

In February 1972, the curator of Greek and Roman art at the Metropolitan Museum received a letter from Robert E. Hecht, Jr., an American dealer in Rome. It asked if the Met would be interested in acquiring a vase equal in value to the Louvre's calyx krater, one of the three greatest pieces of Greek pottery known. Hecht added that the price would be comparable to that of a first-rate Impressionist painting.

Now the Met itself had opened the age of the million-dollar Impressionists with its purchase of Monet's *Terrasse* (at $1,411,200, to be exact) more than two years before, whereas the highest price ever known to have been asked for a vase was $125,000. So when Curator John Cooney of the Cleveland Museum got a similar letter from Hecht, he replied that Cleveland indeed would like to know more about this pot, but he could not imagine asking his trustees to pay anything in six or seven figures. The correspondence, Cooney recounted later, "just petered out." Hecht had a much livelier prospect on his line.

Blond, strong-jawed, blunt and sometimes impatient in speech, with a slight German accent overlaid with Oxford, von Bothmer seemed at first encounter to fit the nickname given him by some colleagues, "the Prussian." The tag is misleading. A former Rhodes scholar from Hitler's Germany, he emigrated to the United States, joined the Army and had an exemplary combat record as an infantryman in the Pacific. On his return, now a naturalized American, he joined the Met to pursue what became an overriding passion — the collection of ancient Athenian pottery. To look at a fine painting on such a vase, he often said, was to be transported back to that glorious age.

What is more, von Bothmer *had* more than a million dollars to spend. Several months earlier, Hoving had ordered his curators to scour their departments for salable art, to replenish funds depleted by the purchase of the Velázquez and other costly works. Von Bothmer came up with the museum's collections of ancient coins. Most of the coins — some 11,000 — had been on loan to the American Numismatic Society uptown, where for more than half a century they had served as a library for historians and students of art and architecture. They bore, among other things, the only existing portraits of many ancient temples, rulers and rites, and their dates were definitive evidence of political and economic events. The Met itself never displayed them, but von Bothmer had paid tribute to their importance and beauty in the catalogue of an exhibition at the coin collectors' society:

> For the collector of Roman antiquities coins are . . . an area in which history and art blend admirably . . . Where else could anybody assemble, with such relative ease, as complete a portrait gallery [of the emperors] as he desires in so small a space, and what other medium combines so many aspects of valuation as rarity, condition and artistic excellence?

But this recognition was for von Bothmer purely intellectual. Coins were not, after all, Athenian vases. When Hoving called for a sacrifice, the curator surrendered the collections with good cheer. They had been, he explained to me later, "a stepchild, a nuisance on my hands."

Although the trustees would not be consulted until June 1972, the decision to sell the coins was actually made in late 1971, and Swiss dealers had been called in that winter to appraise the lot. So when Hecht's letter about the vase arrived in February 1972, von Bothmer already knew that the Greek and Roman coins would fetch more than a million dollars. Unlike Geldzahler in contemporary arts, von Bothmer was not the man to let Hoving pump such money out of his department.

One of the ironies of what followed was that it forced von Bothmer into an alliance with Hoving. The curator had never concealed his low regard for the director. At one of the lavish centennial bashes, von Bothmer had, without troubling to lower his voice, uttered a contemptuous remark as Hoving passed by. Soon thereafter, he was summoned by the director and asked to resign. He refused. Later, he told another curator in the same situation: "The trouble with you is that you never made friends with any trustee." Von Bothmer had powerful friends. He survived.

Hecht's letter held what was bound to excite both men: for von Bothmer, a masterpiece of Attic pottery and, for Hoving, an intrigue in Zurich — the scene of his triumphant "discovery" of the "Bury St. Edmunds" Cross — culminating in a splashy acquisition of great price.

Von Bothmer, Hoving and Chief Curator Theodore Rousseau first saw the vase in a Zurich garden on June 27. Von Bothmer later recalled: "You're prepared for heavenly music, but you don't know how heavenly until you've heard it."

"When I saw the vase," he said, "I knew I had found what I had been searching for all my life."

As a man fond of literary quotations, von Bothmer

might have considered Oscar Wilde's line: "When the gods wish to punish us, they answer our prayers."

What the three men from the Met saw was a much cracked but apparently entire calyx krater, or two-handled bowl for mixing wine and water, of the sixth century B.C. It was eighteen inches high, with ocher figures on black background depicting the dying Sarpedon, son of Zeus, being lifted up by the gods of Sleep and Death. Almost best of all, it was actually signed by the potter Euxitheos and the painter Euphronios, who was one of the two or three greatest masters of Greek vase painting. His surviving works were rare, the last important piece having been found in 1840.

With Dillon's approval, Hoving did not balk at Hecht's price, one million dollars. He ordered the cracks mended and painted over, at the museum's expense. On August 31, Hecht arrived with the vase in a crate and, according to one account, handed it over to Dillon and Hoving at Kennedy International Airport. At any rate, the bill of sale bears that date. The Acquisitions Committee of the trustees approved the purchase twelve days later.

Von Bothmer set to with delight to study the vase and prepare a sumptuous two-color *Bulletin* for a formal unveiling around January. But Hoving suddenly changed the scenario when the scandal over his secret sale of a van Gogh and a Rousseau broke in October. It seemed like a good time to announce a brilliant acquisiton. The director then suggested to trustee Arthur Ochs Sulzberger, publisher of the *Times*, that this would make a fine story for his Sunday *Magazine.**

---

* This is according to Hoving, among others. Because trustees are pledged to secrecy about museum affairs, Sulzberger would have faced a conflict of interest had I questioned him. I never did, nor did he contact me about the Met, directly or indirectly.

The Sunday department of the *Times*, which is independent of, and sometimes in friendly competition with, the news department, assigned a free-lance writer and on November 12 gave the vase as splashy an introduction as ever has been given an art object — something comparable to the opening of the tomb of Tutankhamen. The vase itself made a striking cover, in color, and the story was titillating, if not as informative as it might have been.

Hoving and von Bothmer would not tell where they had got the vase, although they did tell the magazine writer that it had been in a private collection in England about World War I. Nor would they reveal its price, although Hoving did let on that it would be insured for $2,000,000, and "sources close to the Metropolitan" said it cost $1,000,000 in cash and $300,000 in old Greek coins.

Hoving hammered home the link between his sales and his purchases on the "Today" show, with the vase as a prop. Its acquisition, he said, "is the perfect example and the perfect justification for trading out the stuff that we no longer want to show and to put in their place things that indeed will be one of the top pieces in the entire museum, which has three million works of art in it." (His predecessor as director, James J. Rorimer, had put the inventory at 365,000.)

The first question put to him was down-to-earth: "How did you get it, who did you buy it from and how much did it cost?"

"Three of the questions the museum in its crafty way never answers," Hoving replied with zest. "But I'll try to give you some information on it. The poor people have to know about this. We got it from a dealer who was the agent for a person who had this in the family collection since about the First World War, and we don't talk about the name of these people because they have other things that we might want to buy in the future."

Hoving also mailed a card to dues-paying members of the museum, expressing regret that the *Times* scoop had done them out of their right to the first news of this great acquisition. He made up for it with a handsome special edition of the Met's *Bulletin*. His introduction was a specimen of his best lyric prose:

> . . . it is exceedingly rare to acquire a work of art about which one can say unhesitatingly that it is the best in existence, that is one of the two or three finest works of art ever gained by the Metropolitan, and that from this moment — its first public exhibition, now at the Museum — the histories of art will have to be rewritten. Majestic without pomp, poignant without a shred of false emotion, perfect without relying on mere precision, the great krater is one of those rarities.
>
> Appropriately enough, this unsurpassed work of art was acquired with funds obtained through the sale of ancient coins of its realm and time, which had not been on exhibition for many years.

To a collector who observed in a letter that the museum had owned virtually no coins of the "realm and time" of the vase — Athens in the sixth century B.C. — von Bothmer replied, "Perhaps the phrase employed by Mr. Hoving was not a very felicitous one." But the scholars were angry over more than a mere hyperbole.

The specialists had known since spring that a move was afoot to disperse the coin collections, but they had informally agreed to hold their fire while Margaret Thompson of the American Numismatic Society tried to avert what she called a "scholarly disaster," or, failing that, to salvage what she could. Her quiet efforts yielded a gift of $34,000 worth of coins (about 1.5 per cent of the total value) which were returned to the Society as a recompense for sixty-five years of custodianship.*

In its own collecting, the society had never sought duplicates for the coins now suddenly taken away. Miss Thompson raised a modest kitty to bid on some of them in Zurich, but at the first sale in November, speculation by private collectors sent prices so high that all museums were pretty well frozen out. Robert Hecht, incidentally, bought one of the top coins at $40,000.

Miss Thompson recalls an exchange with von Bothmer:

> "All I'm doing is putting the coins back in circulation, which is their original purpose."
>
> "If you'd put your vases back in circulation, I could use your krater for a punchbowl at our next reception."
>
> "Margaret, it leaks."

The first coin auction coincided with the news of the purchase of the Euphronios vase, and both events set off ripples of reprobation among scholars on both sides of the Atlantic. Von Bothmer was the principal target. A Swiss journal, for example, said of his introduction to the sale catalogue: "A complete lack of understanding of the scholarly importance of the coins could hardly be more efficiently demonstrated."

Archaeologists saw the purchase of the vase as a blatant defiance of their long effort to combat the illegal traffic in art. As von Bothmer had observed, Greek pottery was exported in ancient times to specific markets, and the Etruscans had a predilection for Euphronios. It was generally assumed that the krater had come from a new clandestine dig in Etruria, north of Rome.

Some curators were cynical about it. John Cooney of

---

* The trustees eventually canceled the third and final coin auction and sold that lot, consisting of medieval Near Eastern coins, to the society for $150,000. They said nobody had told them the collections had a scholarly value. The two lots sold in Zurich netted the Met $1,770,000.

the Cleveland Museum said: "Unless you're naive or not very bright, you'd have to know that much ancient art here is stolen." His only concern was whether an object had entered the United States legally. "Even if I know it's hot," he elaborated, "I can't be concerned about that. If the museums in this country began sending back all the smuggled material to their countries of origin, the museum walls would be bare."

The "dirt archaeologists" took a different view. Muscarella of the Met recalled: "A dealer once came to me and offered me something from Gordion, the capital city of King Midas. I said, 'But there's a dig there!' He said, 'Dr. Muscarella, I'll give you a pedigree.' He said he was selling stuff to three other departments at the Met without trouble. I threw him out."

Of some twenty archaeologists and curators whom I later canvassed around the country, only one held it at all possible that the Euphronios vase had lain for half a century in a private collection, unknown to scholars. The exception was Cornelius Vermeule, then acting director of the Boston Museum, who, it will be recalled, had bought the gold hoard that had stirred the wrath of Turkey. He was also a close friend of Robert Hecht's. Vermeule told me he thought the story of the English collector was quite plausible, but he was a little miffed at the play it was getting.* He told me what he had told the Boston papers:

---

* Talking earlier to the writer Karl E. Meyer, Vermeule had been more cynical about the discovery of hitherto unknown masterpieces. He said he had made up an all-purpose story about an aristocratic Polish family that was down on its uppers, but had been "somehow able to get its art to the vaults of a Zurich bank."

However, as the scandal of the Euphronios vase mounted, Vermeule grew progressively less loquacious. Toward the end of a conversation in which he had praised the Met's acquisition and the qualities of his friend Hecht — "one of the world's leading authorities on Greek and Roman coins" — I asked Vermeule what he had bought from Hecht.

"I never thought of the publicity potential and brouhaha until I picked up the *New York Times Magazine*, and I said to myself, 'We bought a vase like that, even bigger than theirs — we do things quietly up in Bean Town.' "

Vermeule referred to a krater by the so-called Niobid painter (circa 450 B.C.), which he said he bought from a private American collector early in 1972. "Ours is comparable," he told me, "except that the Met's is signed. The one at the Fogg Museum is not so well preserved, but may be the equal if not the daddy of them all."

(Later, he put it more lyrically, saying that the Fogg vase was "like a ruined Leonardo, the Met's like a perfect Raphael" — although to talk of Raphael in the Boston Museum was like mentioning rope in the house of a hanged man.)

What bothered Vermeule about the Met's acquisition was the price. "Vases aren't Douanier Rousseau's," he said. "There are a considerable number for sale. I bought a wonderful cup, just as beautiful, for $25,000. No vase we've bought in the last decade cost more than one-twentieth of [the million dollars paid by the Met]."

Vermeule recalled evaluating the Fogg Museum's krater at $12,000, for tax purposes, about a decade earlier. Prices had gone up a good deal since then, but the most ever known to have been asked for a vase to date was $125,000. A splendid work by "the Berlin painter," one-third larger than the Met's krater, this vase was shown in 1968 at the André Emmerich Gallery in New York. It was a "breathtaking price," Vermeule recalled, and there were no takers. The krater was returned to Europe, where it was reportedly sold for $100,000.

(I had been tipped that it was Hecht who had sold Boston its Niobid krater.) "I'm trying hard to think," Vermeule replied. "I just can't recall." Thereafter, he declined to accept any further calls from me.

The Met, then, had paid ten times any price hitherto known. But the "dirt archaeologists" were outraged by something more than the likelihood that the Met had been taken for a packet. The newsletter of the Association for Field Archeology said the publication of that incredible price had in one stroke enormously inflated the market for all antiquities, including those already in private collections.

> The purchase [said the newsletter] cannot fail to encourage speculators whose objectives in acquiring ancient art . . . lie in the tax benefits to be saved by donating the objects to museums or educational institutions at their new market value.
> And what of the thieves? Not merely the thieves who may assault the picturesque castles with dusty old private collections, but the brigands whose work has scarred archaeological sites around the world. What visions of quick riches are now conveyed to them by this one transaction!
> As long as acquisition at any price is to be the credo of our major collections, they will fail to serve the cause of knowledge and serve only to incite resentment and encourage crime.

It was in this frame of mind that the diggers went to the annual meeting of the Archeological Institute of America in Philadelphia at the year's end and administered to von Bothmer as stinging a rebuke as ever was received by an American scholar. The curator was on the official slate of six chosen for the board of trustees, a nomination that is normally tantamount to election. From the floor, a seventh nomination was made. Von Bothmer ran seventh, and out.

By a combination of circumstances, the wrath of the scholars escaped the notice of the general public at the time. As noted, those most concerned with the coins had held their fire in vain hopes of negotiating a quiet compromise with Hoving. As for the vase, most of the news media were asleep to the implications of its acquisition.

Not all. Karl E. Meyer began a new chapter of his book *The Plundered Past*. *The Observer* in London, intrigued by the suspicion that a treasure might have been smuggled out of Britain, assigned an investigative team that did a splendid job but, unaware that there was competition on the story, took its time about publishing it. Arthur Gelb, metropolitan editor of *The New York Times*, assigned Nicholas Gage, specialist on organized crime, to track down the origin of the vase, with backup from John Canaday, David Shirey and myself.

It was decided that nothing would be published until the source of the vase could be documented. As a result, when the *Times* broke the story, more than three months after the appearance of the vase, the moral issues were overshadowed by the suspense and comedy of a farcical spy chase. And since the *Times* stayed ahead on this story as it had on the preceding art deals, some rival media were hospitable to Hovings' suggestion that that mighty newspaper was out to get him.

It was nonetheless a marvelous story.

CHAPTER 17

The Chase

I wasted most of my life with whores and archaeologists.

— Dikran Sarrafian to Nicholas Gage

In the gossipy art world, the identity of the "reputable dealer in Switzerland" who had sold the Euphronios vase to the Met did not long remain a mystery. Every curator and dealer in antiquities knew Robert Emmanuel Hecht, Jr. A scion of the Baltimore department store family, he had long been an important supplier to the trade from his home in Rome. His scholarship was respected, but he was not precisely popular. In fact, his temper was widely feared. Classmates recalled fistfights at Haverford College and at the American Academy in Rome. He was *persona non grata* in Turkey, over a matter of some coins he had been carrying on an airplane without an export permit; and he had been accused in Italy of possession of stolen antiquities, but had never been convicted.

Vladimir Stefanelli, who had been helped by Hecht to emigrate to the United States and was now curator of coins at the Smithsonian, told me:

"There are two Hechts. One is the scholar; the other would try to make some sort of success in a more practical field. Bob would give the shirt off his back. But he can become extremely haughty. Then he bores you into the ground, his voice takes on an edge, he tells you unpleasant things. At such moments, he makes enemies."

Stefanelli recalled that he had been questioned about Hecht by the Roman authorities as early as 1950. .

"They read to me certain accusations. They were patently false. They had to do with art objects. But the origin was in some personality conflict . . . Many times people have accused him falsely. Stealing he would not do. Illegal digs — hah! — that's another story."

This, then, was the man who had sold the vase. It remained to prove it. Nicholas Gage, a soft-spoken, pale young reporter with an ulcer, applied the same methodical patience to the task that had distinguished his coverage of the Mafia. Having learned through his colleague Shirey that the vase had been delivered to the Met on August 31, Gage tackled the customs records of shipments to Kennedy Airport that day. There were 16,000 items, but the search could be narrowed down to flights from Switzerland, the *plaque tournante* for traffic in antiquities from the Mediterranean basin. Finally, the paper he was looking for turned up. It showed that a vase valued at $1,000,000 had arrived that day aboard TWA Flight 831 in the company of the "supplier," who was identified as "Robert E. Hecht, Zurich, Switzerland."

Actually, Hecht lived in Rome, but Switzerland, unlike Italy, has no restriction on the export of art objects. So the shipment posed no problem, as far as customs was concerned.

Gage flew to Switzerland and easily established rapport with a number of dealers. He found them engaging and talkative, up to a point. One of them told Gage that, in smuggling antiquities, they were doing the world a service. "Those Greeks, Italians and Turks, what do they know about caring for such pieces? They have no idea how to restore these objects properly. They ruin them. Money is irrelevant to me. What I care about is saving art for posterity." The phone rang. The dealer picked it up, listened, then said: "No, don't bring it by taxi, it will cost too much."

This dealer said the vase had been dug up in late 1971 by clandestine diggers in an Etruscan necropolis thirty-five miles north of Rome, and had been sold to Hecht by a well-known middleman for a bit more than $100,000. The dealer would not identify the middleman, explaining that he, too, did business with "the gentleman."

Gage flew to Rome, where he got the same story. Then he telephoned Hecht and asked for an interview. Hecht invited him to dinner. Gage demurred, but accepted when Hecht insisted he had no other time free. At Hecht's home on the fashionable Aventine Hill near the Forum, the dealer, a middle-aged man with blond hair receding above a triangular face, sat down with his wife and Gage to a frugal meal of pasta, wine, fruit and brownies. It turned out that Gage and Mrs. Hecht both came from Worcester, Massachusetts, and they chatted about that for a while. Then Hecht asked why Gage had come to Rome.

"The Euphronios vase," Gage replied. "Have you seen it?"

"I was in New York three weeks ago. I saw it then."

"Was that the only time you saw it?"

"No, I've seen it before."

Hecht changed the subject. Gage waited, then asked if he had not brought the vase to New York on August 31 aboard TWA flight 831.

Hecht refilled his wine glass.

"Have you seen my tax returns, too?" he asked.

Yes, he acknowledged, he had negotiated the sale of the vase and had delivered it to the Met, but those who said it had been smuggled out of Italy were liars. He had been acting for "a friend, a very nice man," whom Hecht could not identify because it would cause him tax problems in his own country. The vase had been in the man's family for more than fifty years. No, the museum people had never met the collector and had paid the money to Hecht.

"What difference does it make?" he demanded.

Hecht pleaded with Gage not to print the story, because it might mean his expulsion from Rome. His wife, driving the reporter home, added her plea. In the morning, she telephoned to say that Hecht had left Rome, but would have something important to tell him in a couple of days if he would only "hold the presses." It was now Sunday, February 18. Gage filed his story.

In New York, Hoving could not be reached for several days. He was off on a ski trip, it developed. Reached at his weekend home in Syosset, Long Island, von Bothmer said the vase could have come from an English private collection, or it could have come from Italy, "but it doesn't make any difference whether it was the 3198th vase or the 3199th vase found there."

"I want to know where it was made, who did it and when," he said. "I want to know whether it is genuine or fake. Its intermediate history is not important to archaeology. Why can't people look at it simply as archaeologists do, as an art object?"

(This statement shattered most of what was left of von Bothmer's credit among scholars. Margaret Thompson of the American Numismatic Society broke her silence in a letter to the *Times*, saying: "I am outraged . . . any archeologist worthy of the name knows that the place and circumstances of discovery are of great significance for the archeological record." She added that von Bothmer had shown a "similar insensitivity" to scholarship by dispersing a coin collection that in some areas had been unmatched in the Western world.)

The *Times* story caused a sensation in Italy. It developed that the authorities there had been alerted by an inquiry from *The Observer* in London three weeks earlier, and by now they suspected that the vase came from an illegal dig by *tombaroli* — grave robbers — in Etruria in the fall of 1971. Robert Hecht was one of the first persons they had questioned. He told them he knew nothing about it, they said. Now, they asked the United States to look into it.

Back at the Met, von Bothmer was a little more forthcoming. He confirmed that he had first seen the vase on June 27, 1972, in the garden of Fritz Buerki, a restorer who is listed in the Zurich directory as a *sitzmoberschreiner*, or chair mender. The vase had been broken but was complete, except for a few slivers, and had been reassembled. Von Bothmer had said on the "Today" show that he could tell it was genuine "by looking at it, simply by looking at it." Now, he insisted, "I can tell a fake through tissue paper." But he revealed that he had sent some filings from the vase to the thermoluminescence laboratory at Oxford, which determines the age of pottery by measuring the rays it emits when reheated. The test was positive.

At a 1971 conference on the illicit traffic in art, von Bothmer had explained the new policy of the Met: when offered an object "without pedigree," it would first submit a photograph to the authorities of "countries that might consider the object part of their cultural or artistic patrimony." But the problem did not arise here, it appeared, because Hecht did provide a pedigree for the vase. It belonged, he said, to an Armenian dealer named Dikran A. Sarrafian, who lived in Beirut, Lebanon.

"I don't know the man nor anything about him," von Bothmer said. Nor did he ask to meet the man, for as he explained, "There is an etiquette one follows in purchasing art works; if the collector had made up his mind to sell something through a middleman, it means that he doesn't want to be bothered with sales."

But Hecht provided two letters from Sarrafian to him. The first was dated July 10, 1971 — that is, earlier than the Etruscan dig alleged to be the source of the vase. This letter told Hecht: "In view of the worsening situation in the M.E. [Middle East], I have decided to settle in Australia, probably in N.S.W. [New South Wales]. I have been selling off what I have and have decided to sell also my red figured crater which I have had so long and which you have seen with my friends in Switzerland." It mentioned a price of "one million dollars and over if possible" and a commission of 10 per cent for Hecht.

The second letter was dated September 9, 1972, which was nine days *after* the vase had been delivered to the Met. Sarrafian evidently was not aware of the sale and was getting anxious. "Things are hotting up in the M.E. and the situation does not look like improving," he wrote. "So I really do hope and expect that you will effect its sale in the near future."

Sarrafian wrote that the origin of the vase was unknown but his father had "got it by exchange with an amateur against a collection of Greek and Roman gold and silver coins in February or March of 1920 in London." He added: "It was then in fragments and I only authorized its restoration some three years ago."

Von Bothmer said the vase was not yet restored when he had seen it that June, and he had authorized Buerki to fill in the cracks and paint them over at a fee of $800, so that it would be fit to present to the trustees in September. He opined that the vase had been in Switzerland since its purchase in 1920 (the British then had no controls on art exports).

"There would be no reason to take the vase to Lebanon," he explained. "With all the earthquakes and tremors they have there, it was safer in Switzerland."

Gage took the first plane to Beirut and learned that Hecht had been there and was gone. Sarrafian, however, was still around and willing to talk. He did not invite Gage to his home, a modest fourth-floor walkup apartment near the waterfront, but agreed to meet him in the bar of the Hotel St. Georges, a haunt of diplomats, oil men and journalists. Sarrafian was well known there as a small dealer in coins who occasionally promoted "treasure hunts" for tourists at old archaeological sites, with prizes for those who found cheap artifacts he had planted there. Beirut is tolerant, and people rather enjoyed his yarns about imaginary exploits as a British agent in Yugoslavia and Palestine during the war, but nobody took him very seriously. Gage recalls him as "a short, slight man with small black eyes set in a drawn pink face," loquacious but more modest than his reputation — even self-depreciating. Over straight Scotches, he said he was sixty-eight years old and had never accomplished much of anything; he had asked his married children not to follow the Armenian custom of naming their sons after him, because "there is nothing about me worth perpetuating — I wasted most of my life with whores and archaeologists."

He did not collect vases or statues, he said, nor even go out of his way to find them, and when he ran across a good one, he would sell it as soon as possible. He had, however, inherited "a hatbox full of pieces." He hadn't looked at them "for years and years" and had never seen them assembled, but he recalled that they had "paintings of old Greeks and a lot of inscriptions" and that some pieces were missing. (He did not explain how he knew.) "If anyone looks closely at the museum's vase, he should see a lot of painting over," Sarrafian said.

He added that he had never expected the vase to fetch much, and it hadn't — for him.

"Whatever the museum paid, I am not a millionaire. I have no car. I have no yacht. But I am satisfied with what Bob gave me . . . Bob had a nice deal and he made money. I don't begrudge him. I have no complaints. Good luck to him. Only the U.S. Treasury may be the loser, and it lost a lot more in Vietnam."

Sarrafian would not say how much Hecht had paid him, because "money is a personal matter," but said he had no worries about taxes. "Income taxes don't amount to much in Lebanon," he explained.

The dealer confirmed that Hecht had flown to Beirut on Sunday and left the next day. "He came to tell me newspaper people would be calling me," Sarrafian said.

In Zurich meanwhile, callers were told that Buerki the chair mender was away skiing in parts unknown; but Hecht was located at the Hotel Savoie, where he and, incidentally, visitors from the Metropolitan Museum were wont to stay. He said he didn't know anything about the "friends in Switzerland" who, according to the Sarrafian letter, had been keeping the vase for many years. Hecht insisted also that he had paid "the full amount less my commission" to the Lebanese; he offered to show Sarrafian's receipt with the sale price blocked out.

"What I made on it is between Uncle Sam and myself," he said.

Back at the Met, Hoving returned from his ski trip to quell a storm that had been raging for three days. He said he had not previously identified Sarrafian as the seller because the Lebanese owned some other "major objects" and "someone else might jump at them." Hoving had not met the Lebanese, he acknowledged. "What I know about Mr. Sarrafian is what I have heard — that he has some very good things in his collections and that he is a very nice old man."

Hoving said he had received by cable the text of an affidavit sworn by Sarrafian before the United States Consul and, he later added, before the Minister of Justice of Lebanon. It read:

> This is to confirm that the Attic red figure calyx crater signed by Euphronios and consigned by me for sale in Zurich to Mr. Robert E. Hecht Jr. in 1971 formed part of my father's collection and was acquired by him in the winter of 1920 in London in exchange for a collection of gold coins from the Near East. Moreover, the above mentioned crater was in fragments and Mr. Robert Hecht was warned that I was not responsible for any missing pieces.

"I hope that this will shut off all the hot air we have been hearing about the vase," Hoving said. "Only we have produced documents. No one else has."

(In Beirut, the United States consulate had no knowledge of any affidavit by Sarrafian. When the document itself was presented to the press, it turned out to be a letter in English and Arabic, on Sarrafian's stationery, dated February 19, the day of the first *Times* story, when Hecht was in Beirut. It bore a plethora of Lebanese notary stamps. And it was addressed, curiously, to Hecht at the Stanhope Hotel in New York, facing the Metropolitan Museum, where the dealer delivered it to Hoving on Friday in a short secret visit.)

Asked about the "missing pieces" mentioned in the Sarrafian affidavit, Hoving replied: "He undoubtedly was not talking about any major pieces. As ancient vases go, this was in top condition . . . All the vase needed was a little glue and paint in the cracks."

The point was important because the million-dollar price of the krater — ten times the top price believed to have been paid before for a vase — was predicated on its perfect condition. On that assumption, two or three curators were found to consider the vase priceless, but John Cooney of the Cleveland Museum appraised it at $150,000 (adding that he might go up to $250,000); Professor Ross Holloway of Brown University said $200,000 was the limit, and David Owen of the University of Pennsylvania said "a million dollars is absolute nonsense."

"Prices like these are killing antiquities," Owen said. "Every peasant in every little village has heard of high prices and dreams of digging up something that will make him rich for life."

Von Bothmer was plaintive. "Why can't we stop worrying about price?" he said. "Why can't we just appreciate the vase for what it is: a glorious object with brilliant colors and an extraordinary composition? It is one of the great works of antiquity and should be looked at as such."

The fact that the vase had been broken into many parts was significant for another reason, which up to this writing has never been publicly remarked. There are ten human figures on the krater; not one of the breaks crosses any of the ten faces. If this occurred by accident, it was almost miraculous. It would be more understandable if, as frequently happened, an experienced operator had deliberately broken up the vase to facilitate smuggling it out of Italy.

The Italian police were working on the smuggling hypothesis. It was announced that four unidentified men had been officially advised to engage defense counsel, a procedure under Italian law preliminary to a criminal inquiry. Acting on a tip, Gage and an interpreter drove twenty miles northwest of Rome to Cerveteri, and went from door to door asking for a man nicknamed *il Ciccione*. They were finally directed to a two-room stone house, where they found a short, husky, unshaven man in bare feet. He was Armando Cenere, a sometime farm laborer and mason, who readily confirmed that when jobs were scarce, as they often were, he would join teams of *tombaroli* in digging among the thousands of Etruscan tombs in the area.

Seated by the stove, Cenere told this story. He was one of six men digging nearby at Santangelo in mid November 1971, when they turned up the base and handle of a Greek vase. He was detailed as lookout while the men cleared and cleaned out an underground tomb. The job took a week, and the loot was big. It included many pieces of pottery, and a winged sphinx; the men decided to leave the sphinx in the field and then tip off the police, so as to allay suspicion.

Cenere particularly recalled a piece of pottery about the size of a hand, with the figure of a man bleeding from three wounds. From a photograph of the Metropolitan's vase (after restoration), he identified the portrait of the dying Sarpedon, and with a crayon drew a line above the knees where it had been broken. He said the leaders of the gang had eventually paid him 5,500,000 lire (about $8800) as what they called an equal share of the booty. Because he had learned that one vase alone had fetched enormously more, he had willingly told the authorities what he knew.

Gage and his interpreter, another frail, scholarly type, headed back to Rome. On the way, as Gage told it later in a *Times* house organ:

> A few miles out of Cerveteri, in the best Mafia style a large red car overtook us and forced us off the road. Two sinister-looking men got out and walked toward us while I cursed Euphronios and Editor Arthur Gelb.
>
> It turned out they were only friendly natives eager to help us out. They knew we weren't really newspapermen, they said, but officials from the American museum, and for

a fee they would be glad to testify in any way that would help us keep the vase. At that point, the police arrived, wanting to know why we had stopped on a freeway. We apologized and took off for Rome.

Cenere's testimony was not conclusive, of course. He could have been mistaken, or he could have been making up the whole story, or part of it — for example, the vase might have been carefully broken *after* it had been found, so as to conceal it more easily. But Hoving chose to call it a frame-up, organized by the *Times*.

He said first that Cenere's description "does not seem to agree with what we know definitively about the fragments, as anybody can see by looking at the actual piece." Further, there was the Sarrafian affidavit. "I don't take sworn statements lightly," he said, "especially statements made before a Minister of Justice." Then in an interview with young David Shirey of the *Times*, a friend of years' standing, he raised his tone in a manner that left Shirey shaken. He charged that the *Times* had radioed to Gage a photograph that the Met had lent Shirey, showing the cracked vase before restoration. This, Hoving said, had been shown to Cenere. He threatened to sue for libel.

In fact, the photo in question showed only the back of the vase. It had not been radioed to Italy. Nor did Hoving sue.

An archaeologist telephoned me with a new revelation. He had attended the year-end meeting of the Archeological Institute of America that closed with the defeat of von Bothmer. At an earlier session, the curator had given a talk on the myth of Sarpedon, illustrated with slides of its portrayal by the artist Euphronios. What the audience saw was not only the scene on the calyx krater, but also an earlier treatment of the subject on a lovely little kylix cup — a second, hitherto unknown work by Euphronios.

It was only when he read that the police, acting on information from the *tombaroli*, were looking for a second fine vase and a Euphronios cup with a dying warrior scene that the archaeologist realized the significance of what he had seen.

Sadly and wearily, von Bothmer confirmed the story. He did have a photograph of the Euphronios cup, he told me, but he "wouldn't know" who owned it, nor comment on where it had come from.

"There is no source to a cup," he said. "A cup is a cup."

Where was it now?

"It's supposed to be in Norway."

What was it worth?

"I am an archaeologist, not an appraiser.'

No, he could not release a copy of the photograph, since the owner might have a prior claim to it. Deploring the harassment of the news media, von Bothmer then sadly quoted the line of the poet Flecker about "Broken vases widowed of their wine."

"Euphronios had only one rival, Euthemides," von Bothmer said. "He once wrote on a vase, 'unlike anything Euphronios ever did.' I tell myself that somewhere behind this is Euthemides, trying to get even."

For his part, Hoving told Shirey, he had never seen the cup or a photograph of it, and had never considered buying it. Later, he telephoned and said: "I want to be perfectly clear that I never saw the cup. I did see a photograph."

Hoving had perhaps suddenly recalled an interview he had granted to Richard Walter of *The Observer* on February 14, five days before the first Gage story on the vase. Walter had taken the precaution to tape their chat. Hoving was talkative, in the manner of Casey Stengel.

"Funny thing is," he said, "I was offered today a kylix thing, shaped like that, a wine jug, whatever you call it —

kylix — by Euphronios, signed by him, in bad fragments, in pieces but many great lumps missing, and the subject is the carrying off the dead body of Sarpedon by Sleep and Death done about twenty years before this, the krater, by the same man — totally different, stiff, awkward-looking in the old tradition — so we hope maybe we can acquire it . . .

"The price is not very high* — it's just minuscule compared to the price of the calyx krater, but it still is, for the fragmentary condition of the thing, well, it's a bit, well, off the record, it should be around [deleted] and it's more than that — and he's not trying to go gaga on it, but it's just a little bit off so, because it is, if I had the photograph, which I don't, I sent it back. It is really ripped apart. Maybe we get someone to divide and give it to us."

Two days later, Walter talked to von Bothmer, who said the cup was ten years older than the vase, not twenty, and he'd rather not talk much about it because "I very much want to buy it."

"I don't want to have an exclusive on Sarpedon," he said. "On the other hand, it would mean so much more to me."

WALTER: I thought I understood that both came from the same — that they were both being handled by the same person?

VON BOTHMER: That is one of those extraordinary coincidences, but it is literally, once again, a coincidence. [Pause.] There are coincidences in life and I want to make the most of them. In this case, I really do want to get this piece.

WALTER: Isn't it a good fortune for Robert Hecht as

---

* *The Observer* and American museum sources said the cup was being offered at $15,000, a far cry indeed from the price of the vase.

well, that he manages to have first the vase and then the cup?

VON BOTHMER: The other way round — the cup has been owned for a couple of years. I saw this cup in July 1971. [Pause.] I stopped in Zurich and I saw the cup and I have my notes and my dates. I would put it differently — the cup at the price then being quoted me was not nearly so exciting to me until after this object [the vase] appeared. Therefore, when you have two of a kind, it takes on greater significance.

Thus, when von Bothmer talked to Walter on February 16, he thought the vase had been found sometime *after* July 1971, when he saw the cup in Zurich. He was presumably aware of Sarrafian's letters to Hecht, saying the vase had been in his family for more than fifty years. But he was not aware that the Italian police would date its discovery as mid November 1971.

Speaking to the *Times* ten days later, von Bothmer rolled back the date. He said it had taken Fritz Buerki, the chair mender, twelve months to restore the vase. Returning to Zurich from his holiday, Buerki confirmed this by telephone. He said he had received the vase in the summer of 1971, and it had already been restored, but "so badly that I had to take it to pieces and restore it again." (It was never explained why the process took so long; when von Bothmer saw it in June 1972 it had only been assembled for viewing, cracks and all, and Buerki had at most two months more to complete the job.)

In New York, Hoving said he now had a sworn statement from Buerki that Sarrafian had given him the vase in August 1971. Hoving had presumably received this document along with the Sarrafian affidavit from Robert Hecht, who had flown from Zurich two days earlier for a hasty visit. Hoving revealed that he too had seen the vase in Zurich in the summer of 1972. The first thing he asked Hecht about it, he said, was the price.

"Mr. Hecht asked for a lot more than $1,000,000," Hoving reported. "He said that the beauty of the Euphronios krater was that it had a good provenance, and that you have to pay for that kind of thing.

"The next thing I asked him was whether it was a hot pot. I wanted to make sure that we were buying the vase in good faith. Mr. Hecht said that the krater was definitely not a hot pot. We had no reason to doubt him. We had dealt with him before and never had any trouble. Mr. Hecht has one of the best eyes in the business. He's the kind of guy whose opinion I would ask on an ancient work."*

A telephone call by Shirey found Hecht back at the Hotel Savoie in Zurich. How long he would stay, he said, "depends on the Italian police — I want to see if they plan to give me free room and board."

Hecht added that he had planned to give the *Times* a "major statement" when he was in New York, but had been talked out of it by Hoving, his vice director, Theodore Rousseau, and by his own lawyer.

The dealer now remembered meeting some Lebanese friends of Sarrafian's in Zurich back in 1971 and being taken by them to Buerki's house to see the vase. He also now hedged on the terms of his deal with Sarrafian. "The final agreement between us was different than the original one," he said. "Mr. Sarrafian says what he has to say. We each have our own treasury."

---

* An archaeologist at the University of Pennsylvania, Keith DeVries, wrote the *Times*, that this was "like praising Fagin for his deep appreciation of silk handkerchiefs."

Hecht also explained his sudden departure from Rome, the morning after he had dined with Gage.

"I had to go to Beirut anyway. While I was there, I also saw Mr. Sarrafian. I told him that some journalists were doing a smear job on the sale of the vase.

"I've known Sarrafian for more than fifteen years. He is the greatest gentleman. He is sophisticated. He went to a Quaker school and he served with the British Intelligence. He likes fine foods and wine. It burned me up that some shoddy sensationalist would want to blacken his reputation . . .

"I believe in God, I believe in decency and integrity, I believe in Sarrafian."

His faith was no longer requited. In Beirut, Sarrafian told *The Observer:*

"Bob was clever, I was stupid. I wouldn't have given him an invoice for the vase — one dealer doesn't usually give an invoice to another — but he specifically asked for one. He said he wanted it for tax purposes . . . I gave him an invoice saying he had paid a fantastic price for the vase. I didn't get even one quarter of a million dollars for it. The bulk of the money went to Hecht. The amount of tax he will pay is minimal, and I shall have all the troubles with the authorities."

The ties of loyalty at the Metropolitan Museum proved stronger. At his home in Hobe Sound, Florida, President Dillon granted a telephone interview — his first in a year of scandals involving the Met. The acquisition of the Euphronios vase was completely legal and done in good faith, he declared.

"Ever since Mr. Hoving supported the resolutions of the UNESCO convention," he said, "we have been particularly conscious of illicit traffic in art."

He conceded that the trustees, in considering the pur-

chase of an object, were perhaps "more interested in looking at it as a work of art then verifying its provenance."

"It's not up to the trustees to check on provenance," he
said. They are usually not art experts. They depend on
the director and the curator for that information."

Hoving had provided more than adequate supporting data
on the vase, Dillon indicated — "in fact, I don't think that
on some objects in the museum we have a dossier as exten-
sive as the one we have on the vase."

Hoving now added another item to the dossier. In a
radio interview, he explained the million-dollar price this
way: "We knew there were private collectors who would
be willing to pay instead of $1,000,000 perhaps $800,000,
but that would have meant that it would have been in a
private collection in Germany or Switzerland or England,
and the United States and New York would never have had
it. The Metropolitan does sometimes have to pay a pre-
mium, because we are the great one of the United States,
and the right of first refusal sometimes costs a bit more,
but again, that's part of the curious nature of the business."

Hoving never identified the other bidders for the vase,
nor did the banker Dillon comment on the necessity of the
Met's paying more than a private collector would.

Recalling Hoving's past political ambitions, the interviewer asked if he might be considering running for mayor
or something. He did not rule it out. He replied:

"Well, I'm the last of the old breed of grand acquisitors
of works of art. I've done it since 1959, and I guess per-
sonally tally up about a quarter of a billion dollars that has
come into the Metropolitan in works of art since then, and
I'll probably stick with the Metropolitan through this par-
ticular kerfuffle, you know, and stick with it until this is
cleared up, which I'm sure is going to be cleared up in our
favor, but I —"

"You mean that there's a chance that you may leave the Met after this is cleared up?" the interviewer asked.

"Well, sooner or later. One of these years, I suppose, you've got to hand it over to younger, less tired people, but my métier in life, my job in life has always been collecting and trying to get these extraordinary pieces for the City of New York, and I must say it's getting more difficult every day."

The tired acquisitor was now forty-two years old. He had said much the same thing more than three years earlier, in the wake of the kerfuffle over the *Harlem on My Mind* show. He had suggested at the time that his job of rebuilding the Met should not take more than five or six years, all told, and in 1973 that term would run out.

But there was no sign that the trustees would be willing to let him set down the burden. Hoving now put their faith to an even greater test. The Italian police had raided the home of an accused *tombarolo* in Cerveteri and seized fragments of ancient Greek pottery, and also recovered other shards from the tomb thought to be the source of the Euphronios vase and cup. Through Interpol, they sought photographs of the vase before it had been restored, and of the cup, and other data in possession of the Met. The F.B.I. and the New York City police put the request to Hoving. "On advice of counsel" he declined. He also refused to allow experts to study the vase with ultraviolet rays and other techniques to learn how much restoration had been done and whether the cracks were new or ancient.

Hoving explained that he did not want to hinder the truth from coming out in any Italian court proceeding. He reiterated that the *Times* in its vendetta against him had already radioed "pre-restoration photographs" to Europe. In several interviews he insisted that Cenere, the *tombarolo*, had been briefed with such photographs.

Hecht had told the *Times* he was ready to buy back the vase for a million dollars plus interest. But Hoving ignored the chance. As the weeks went by, his confidence grew. He told Barbara Goldsmith of *New York* magazine:

"Our case is airtight. Italy will never get the krater back. Even if they win their case, our UNESCO agreement states that they'd have to pay our price. That's a million dollars, and last year they raised about $37.75 to save *all* of Venice, and that was in *lire*."

Whither the Museum?

> Because the city puts monies into keeping this place
> up, there can be an easy confusion on the part of the
> general taxpayer that he somehow owns pieces of the
> art in this institution. The facts are, he doesn't. But he
> *believes* he does, and it has become a Pirandellian reality.
> It is as it appears to be. It's a straight Pirandello thing,
> and the public's got the power of that behind it right
> now, so it becomes a different and a more powerful force
> than it used to be.
>
> — Thomas Hoving, in an interview with
> *New York* magazine

There is no happy ending. The hot pot might eventually
be restored to Italy, or it might not; the last wishes of
Adelaide Milton de Groot might be respected, or they
might not; official investigators might seek to resolve
whether there had been corruption as well as folly in the
dealings of the Metropolitan Museum of Art, or they might
not; the trustees might finally decide to rid themselves of
the permanent kerfuffle that is Hoving, or they might not.
But such action or failure to act would not touch the
fundamental question raised by six years of Metropolitan
scandals: in a free society, who shall control the museums?

It may seem an exaggeration to call the Hoving regime
typical of American museums in general, but a caricature is
one way of describing the normal. Other museums had
their secret scandals, but none had been the object of a
sustained inquiry by the press.

The art world immediately recognized that all of it was involved in the mess at the Met. Each segment reacted according to its nature. The artists, supreme individualists, for the most part looked on sardonically, although at one point an extremist fringe went apicketing and even tossed cockroaches on the festive table at a party in the Met. The world of scholarship represented in the College Art Association and other organizations, roundly denounced the depredations of the Hoving regime and demanded a voice in future sales and acquisitions. The art dealers criticized the abuses that had been exposed, and offered their services to help regulate the market in museum art so as to minimize scandals in the future — just as they had volunteered to help limit the tax racket in the overappraisal of art donated to museums. (That way, they staved off a more serious reform. Museums are still excellent tools for tax avoidance and for the enhancement of private collections through their exhibition on loan.)

The Establishment, for the most part, held its silence. In other cities, museum directors and trustees sought to assure their clientele that what was happening at the Met was strictly a New York aberration, like mugging. In New York itself, people of influence sought to keep the lid on, to work out some small measure of reform, and if possible a dignified exit from the crisis, without reducing their authority and above all without reflecting on the wisdom of the Establishment.

Bills were introduced in the state legislature and the City Council to require museums supported by public funds to notify the public before disposing of art. Feeble as the proposals were, they were shelved in committee. A symbolic motion in the City Council to delete a budget appropriation of $312,000 for a new roof for the Met was defeated, 26 to 10. At a budget hearing, Councilman

Carter Burden bitterly told a black delegation seeking a small subsidy for a neighborhood museum that there were no city funds for them. On the other hand, he said, there *were* city funds for "an institution that spends five and a half million dollars for one picture and a million dollars for a Greek vase."

Throughout the scandals, Mayor Lindsay and Governor Rockefeller had no comment. A stand was taken, however, by the new Commissioner of Parks, Recreation and Cultural Affairs, Richard M. Clurman. In an eloquent article on the Op-Ed page of *The New York Times*, he appealed to the citizenry not to force the museums to give advance notice of their buying and selling. Not to him, anyway; he had no intention of becoming "Cultural Commissar of New York."

Clurman said he favored more, not less, government aid to the arts, but less, not more, government management of the arts.

> The city is for the most part the landlord of organizations who have been adjudged worthwhile and whose main support comes from the private sector. The city nominally owns Joe Papp's Public Theater, but should it criticize his productions? The city, indeed, owns the Bronx Zoo. Should it tell the New York Zoological Society that it must stock more (or less) indigenous birds of New York City? The City owns the Metropolitan Museum of Art's building and helps maintain it with an annual capital and operating contribution. Should the city therefore assess the price and value of a Velazquez as compared to using those assets for, perhaps, commissioning new portraits by Norman Rockwell of the Mayor's cabinet? . . .
>
> Whatever the arrogance of Tom Hoving or the guerrilla-like determination of Joe Papp, I would much prefer to take my artistic chances with them and their organizations rather than entrust the conduct of our cultural affairs to the legis-

lated power of a Dick Clurman or the esthetic opinions of the officials who make up the City Council and Board of Estimate.

Clurman ended by reproaching John Canaday of the *Times* for taking time out from "the paper's pursuit of the Metropolitan, as if it were the Mafia," to suggest that some degree of official supervision might be in the offing and that the trustees had brought it upon themselves. The commissioner said the press, rightly alarmed at "governmental invasion of its freedom, might well bellow at those who would urge elected and appointed officials — including me — to mess in the artistic management of our cultural institutions."

A strong argument, well put. Clurman neglected, however, to mention that he was himself a trustee of the Met, ex officio, as were the mayor and the city controller, and hence obliged by law to oversee the artistic judgments of the director and to guard the treasure of the museum. Like the other trustees, he was copping out.

The comparison of Joseph Papp to Thomas Hoving was hardly appropriate. Papp was an artist of proved integrity and performance. Further, like any artist, he put his reputation on the line with every production. If he were to destroy the credit of his theater with a series of esthetic and moral disasters over the years, surely *somebody* would do something about it. Nobody can force the public to subsidize bad conduct forever.

By contrast, a museum director may pretend expertise in all areas of art and get away with it indefinitely; in the land of the blind trustee, as we have said, the one-eyed man is king. Hoving could build a reputation for scholarship on the fictitious "discovery" and dubious "identification" of the so-called Bury St. Edmunds Cross. His vice director, Theodore Rousseau (who bought the absurd rocking-chair

"Velázquez"), could deny the authenticity of an Ingres or a Modigliani. Von Bothmer, the passionate collector of Athenian vases, could go along with Hoving in branding the Greek *Bronze Horse* a modern fake, and then retreat to calling it an ancient Roman one. Curator Everett Fahy, the brilliant specialist on Italian Renaissance paintings, could go along with Hoving on the Ingres, and then recant. And they could all get away with it, indefinitely.

Clurman's comparison of the cultural institutions to the press is equally far-fetched. Newspapers and book publishers are not subsidized (except for bargain mail rates, which are contestable). Museums *are* subsidized. Clurman was of course in error when he said "their main support comes from the private sector." Through tax deductions, tax exemptions and direct subsidies (not to mention paid admissions), it is quite evidently the general public that gives these institutions their main support.

A truism is expressed in a cultural metaphor: who pays the piper calls the tune. This is not so, however, for those cultural institutions that are paid by the public but ruled by self-perpetuating boards of trustees. It is often said that this system has endowed the United States with a magnificent network of museums. Granted. So was the nation endowed with a great railroad network in the age of the Robber Barons, the grandparents of our present trustees. But that system of private control of a public service, carried over to our day, led to bankruptcy.

The country is not now prepared to take over directly the burden of running all its cultural institutions. But there is a growing awareness of the abuses committed by tax-exempt foundations, including museums, and it is inevitable that further supervision will be called for. The scandals of the Met can only promote this trend.

Clurman raised a real problem, to which he had no

answer. One may agree that he is not qualified to pass on the purchase or sale of a Velázquez. Neither is Douglas Dillon, or Hoving. But as parks commissioner, Clurman is not required to be an expert on chrysanthemums. He *is,* however, required to try to engage qualified experts to do the work and to insure that the public's money is spent honestly.

Neither he nor his employees may conceal their transactions from the public. They must advertise contracts and award them to the highest bidders. Their salaries are on the public record. By contrast, none but a few insiders are privy to the salaries paid by the city-subsidized museum of which Clurman is landlord and trustee (Hoving's salary is rumored to be far above the Mayor's); the director of the Met could, by his own boast, acquire, sell or swap a quarter of a billion dollars' worth of art without a word to the public about the terms of the dealings, or even the fact that they had occurred.

Clearly, this situation cannot endure. If they are to keep their tax exemptions and subsidies, our museums will have to conduct their affairs in the broad daylight of public scrutiny.

It is just as clear that wealth and social status are not sufficient qualifications for the trusteeship of tax-supported institutions. No doubt the generous collector-donor can still play a useful role, but a majority of the places should go to artists, scholars, curators and representatives of the public elected periodically by their constituencies.

Finally, the professional staff of a museum should in practice as well as in principle enjoy the same rights to tenure and the same voice in policy as the faculty of a properly run university.

Such reforms would give us neither a commissariat of culture nor a fiefdom, but a democratic regime. Democracy being an imperfect form of government, it should not be expected to solve all the problems. But if, then, we ran into new scandals of the kind that have plagued the Metropolitan Museum of Art, we would have only ourselves to blame.